The Reference Guide to

DATA SOURCES

ALA Editions purchases fund advocacy, awareness, and accreditation programs for library professionals worldwide.

The Reference Guide to DATA SOURCES

JULIA BAUDER

An imprint of the American Library Association

CHICAGO 2014

Julia Bauder is the social studies and data services librarian at the Grinnell College Libraries in Grinnell, Iowa. Bauder holds a master's degree from the School of Library and Information Science at Wayne State University in Detroit, Michigan. Before becoming a librarian, she spent several years as a freelance writer and editor of reference books.

Printed in the United States of America

18 17 16 15 14 5 4 3 2 1

ISBNs: 978-0-8389-1227-0 (paper); 978-0-8389-1962-0 (PDF); 978-0-8389-1963-7 (ePub); 978-0-8389-1964-4 (Kindle). For more information on digital formats, visit the ALA Store at alastore.ala.org and select eEditions.

Library of Congress Cataloging-in-Publication Data

Bauder, Julia.
The reference guide to data sources / Julia Bauder.
p. cm.
Includes bibliographical references and index.
ISBN 978-0-8389-1227-0 (alk. paper)
1. Statistics—Computer network resources—Handbooks, manuals, etc. 2. Social sciences—Statistics—Handbooks, manuals, etc. 3. Internet research—Handbooks, manuals, etc. 4. Electronic reference sources—Handbooks, manuals, etc. 5. Internet searching—Handbooks, manuals, etc. 6. World Wide Web—Subject access—Handbooks, manuals, etc. I. Title. II. Title: Guide to data sources.
HA33.5.B38 2014
025.06—dc23 2014006175

Cover design by Alejandra Diaz. Image ©bloomva/Shutterstock, Inc.

Text design in the Chaparral, Gotham, and Bell Gothic typefaces.

♾ This paper meets the requirements of ANSI/NISO Z39.48-1992 (Permanence of Paper).

Contents

Acknowledgments *ix*

1 | **Data Reference Basics** *1*

2 | **General Sources** *13*

3 | **Agriculture and Food** *21*

4 | **Crime** *27*

5 | **Earth Science—General** *31*

6 | **Earth Science—Air, Climate, and Weather** *37*

7 | **Earth Science—Water** *43*

8 | Economics—General 47

9 | Economics—Government Finance 51

10 | Economics—Firms and Industries 55

11 | Economics—Commodities 61

12 | Economics—Labor 65

13 | Economics—Macroeconomic Accounts 71

14 | Economics—Banks and Lending 75

15 | Economics—Real Estate 81

16 | Economics—Trade and Tariffs 85

17 | Education 93

18 | Energy 99

19 | Health and Health Care 103

20 | People and Households 111

21 | Political Science—Elections 119

22 | Political Science—War and Peace 125

23 | Political Science—Other 129

24 | Public Opinion Surveys 133

25 | Transportation *137*

26 | Spatial Data *143*

27 | When All Else Fails: Using Article Databases, WorldCat, and Real Live People to Find Data *147*

Appendixes

A Citing Data *151*

B Getting Started with the Survey Documentation and Analysis Software *155*

Index *161*

Acknowledgments

THANK YOU TO ANNE O'DWYER FOR INTRODUCING ME TO QUANTITATIVE research in the social sciences, and to all of the faculty at Simon's Rock College who worked so hard to help me become a better writer. I would not have been able to write this book without their patient teaching.

Thank you to Alana Joli Abbott for setting me up with my first freelance writing jobs, which started me on the career trajectory that led to this book.

Thank you to all of the data librarians who graciously welcomed me into the profession. This list includes Chuck Humphrey and Jim Jacobs, whose ICPSR class, Providing Social Science Data Services: Strategies for Design and Operation, was an excellent introduction to the field, and my colleagues in the International Association for Social Science Information Services and Technology and the ACRL Numeric and Geospatial Data Services in Academic Libraries Interest Group.

Thank you to the countless people over the years who have said to me, "Hey, have you seen this great data set?" I first became aware of many of the sources listed in this book because an enthusiastic colleague shared them with me, and I appreciate both the tips and the enthusiasm.

Thank you to Grinnell College for generously funding research leaves for junior faculty, including me, and to all of my colleagues in the Grinnell College Libraries who picked up the slack for me while I was off writing. I would never have had the time to write this book without that support.

Thank you to the wonderful editorial team at ALA Editions. They provided excellent suggestions that improved this book immensely.

And, finally, thank you to all of my friends and family who, for almost a year, put up with me saying, "I can't; I have to write!"

1 Data Reference Basics

QUESTIONS ABOUT STATISTICS—"WHAT IS THE POPULATION OF London?" "How many people are diagnosed with cancer annually?"—have long been a staple at library reference desks. Most librarians are familiar with the print ready-reference sources that were traditionally kept within reach to answer them—the *Statistical Abstract of the United States, The World Almanac and Book of Facts,* and the *CIA World Factbook,* to name just a few—and, now, with the online equivalents of these publications. Not too many years ago, however, "data reference" was a specialized library service available primarily at research libraries. Few librarians outside of those institutions would ever encounter a question like "I need thirty years of time-series data on the production of beef in Texas at the county level," and even fewer librarians would have been comfortable with the intricacies of working with data on reel-to-reel tapes and punchcards.

Two changes—the rise of the Internet, which has made disseminating data much less complicated, and the spread of statistical software packages into the undergraduate curriculum—have blurred the line between statistics reference and data reference. As more data and more user-friendly tools to work with data have become available, interest in finding and using quantitative data has grown. Yet data-related reference questions are often some of the most daunting questions for general reference librarians. My hope is that this guide makes those questions a little less daunting.

FOR WHOM IS THIS GUIDE INTENDED?

Although I hope that all reference librarians find this guide helpful, its primary audience is librarians at public libraries, high school libraries, and the majority of academic libraries that do not employ staff dedicated to data reference. Librarians working with undergraduates at large research institutions may also find that the guide allows them to answer some basic data reference questions without having to refer students to a dedicated data services librarian.

Because the intended audience is primarily librarians at institutions that have not made a major financial commitment to data services, this guide focuses on freely available, online sources for data. In many subject areas, much of the most frequently used data can be found online for free if one knows where to look. On the occasions when a commonly requested type of data is not freely available from any online source, subscription databases or print series containing the data may be mentioned. Librarians whose institutions subscribe to many statistical databases may find Lynda M. Kellam's guide *Numeric Data Services and Sources for the General Reference Librarian* (Chandos, 2011), which focuses more on subscription databases for data reference, to be helpful for their situation.

This guide focuses on data available through English-language interfaces, although it occasionally makes reference to data available in foreign-language interfaces. It does not include certain specialized scientific data sources, such as gene sequence databases or databases of chemical structures; nor does it include qualitative data sources. Instead, the focus is on quantitative social science data, broadly defined—that is, data that is primarily useful in the context of social science disciplines such as economics and sociology, as well as scientific data that frequently is or can be deployed in the context of government policy making, such as data on public health, climate change, or natural disasters.

In the following thematic chapters 2–26, the discussion is divided into three categories: major sources for U.S. data, major sources for international data, and minor sources. The sites listed as major sources are large databases, typically from the major international or federal government agencies with responsibility for a given area; they are the most likely resources for answering most common reference questions in their areas.

Minor sources were selectively chosen from the dozens of smaller data sources in each area because they fill a gap in the data that is available from the major sources or because they present a selection of data from the major sources in a more user-friendly interface.

DATA JARGON

To communicate with patrons who need data, and to get the most out of the rest of this book, it helps to be aware of certain types of data jargon. As with any kind of reference question, before undertaking a search for data it is important to be sure you understand exactly what your patrons want. In the case of data that means understanding not only exactly the topic on which they need data but also the characteristics of the data they need: whether they need *statistics* or *data*, what their desired *universe* and *unit of analysis* are, whether they want *time series* or *cross-sectional* data, and more. The italicized terms, and other related concepts, are defined below.

Data versus Statistics

The terms *data* and *statistics* are often used as if they mean the same thing (sometimes even in this book), but in fact there is an important distinction between them. Data is raw input for some sort of statistical analysis. A list of all of the traffic accidents in New Jersey in 2010, with information about the drivers (e.g., age, blood alcohol content, whether they were using a cell phone at the time of the accident) and the accident (e.g., time of day, weather, number of cars involved) would be data. Unless you are interested in information about a specific accident (say, if you are a lawyer representing one of the drivers), this list is not likely to be terribly informative by itself. To be able to say anything about road safety in New Jersey generally, you would need statistics. Statistics, in this context, are the results of a statistical analysis of the data. *Statistical analysis* does not have to mean some sort of complicated multivariate regression. In many cases, it is simply an average, a percentage, or a frequency. For example, the percentage of accidents that occur during snowstorms, or the frequency of accidents involving teenage drivers, are examples of statistics that could be generated from this data.

Certain pieces of information can be treated as either statistics or data, depending on what the user wants to do with that information. Take, for example, the unemployment rate of the United States in November 1980: 7.5 percent, according to the Bureau of Labor Statistics.[1] This number is a statistic—the product of statistical analysis of the data gathered from individuals in the labor force by the Current Population Survey—and, for a history student writing a paper about how economic conditions affected the 1980 presidential race, it might be all that he needs. However, an economics student who wants to test the hypothesis that changes in the price of oil affect the unemployment rate in the United States might treat that same number as a data point: one of many monthly unemployment rates that she will use to run regressions, thereby generating other statistics.

Subtypes of Data: Microdata and Aggregate Data

The term *microdata* is used to refer specifically to the kind of data that is, unequivocally, data rather than statistics: raw observations, survey responses, and the like that are not the product of any kind of statistical analysis or summary. *Microdata* often refers to data about individual people. A spreadsheet where each row contains a single person's responses to the questions on a survey is an example of microdata. The traffic accident data mentioned above would also be considered microdata, as would information about individual stores collected as part of the Economic Census or daily rainfall totals for a specific location as reported by the National Weather Service.

The converse of microdata is *aggregate data*—data produced by some sort of statistical procedure, such as averaging or, in the most basic and perhaps the most common example, simply adding up the number of cases. Monthly unemployment rates are an example of what might be referred to as aggregate data, as are election results by precinct and data about retail establishments by county. If the description of a data table ends with "by state," "by gender," or something similar, you are almost certainly dealing with aggregate data.

Public-Use Data versus Restricted Data

In this book, I try to focus on freely available data, where "freely" means two different things: that no monetary payments are required to access the data, and that there are no onerous restrictions on who may have access to the data or the conditions under which they may use the data. Nevertheless, some of the resources mentioned in this book contain both *public-use data* (data with either no restrictions at all on access or with minimal registration requirements) and *restricted data* (data for which access is conditional and requires an approval process). Accessing restricted data may be as simple as filling out a short online form and waiting for approval, or it may be as complicated as completing an extensive certification process and traveling to a designated data enclave (a secure facility with equipment and policies designed to prevent the unauthorized sharing of confidential information) to use the data.

Why is some data public-use and other data restricted? The section "What Data Is Not Disseminated?" (p. 10) explains how concerns about privacy and confidentiality can lead to restrictions on data access.

Surveys, Censuses, and Administrative Data

Surveys are one of the most common methods of gathering data in the social sciences. In a survey, data is gathered from a *sample* (a small subset) of the population (sometimes called the *universe*), and that data is then used to make estimates about the entire population. For example, a typical public opinion survey might do telephone interviews with one thousand people (the sample) randomly selected from all adults over 18 years of age who reside in the United States (the universe). These thousand people's responses would then be used to estimate how the entire adult population of the United States feels about, say, the president's job performance. This contrasts with a *census*, which is often conducted like a survey in that people are asked to answer questions over the telephone or to fill out a form, but, instead of contacting a sample of the population, the goal with a census is to contact every single person (or, in the case of the Economic Census, the Census of Agriculture, or the Census of Jails, every single institution) in the population. It also contrasts with *administrative data*—in which official records (say, birth certificates, tax returns, or customs declaration forms) are used to gather data, rather than asking people or institutions directly to provide information about themselves.

Cross-Sectional, Longitudinal, and Time-Series Data

Many studies gather data at only a single point in time: a survey is written, people respond to it over a few days or weeks, the data is analyzed, and then the study is complete. This type of data is relatively cheap and easy to gather, but it is difficult or impossible to use it to examine changes over time. These types of studies are called *cross-sectional* studies or surveys. Because so many studies are cross-sectional, the types of data that are collected over time are more challenging to find. However, because they can be used to do more sophisticated types of analyses, they are particularly valuable to researchers.

The two main types of data that have been collected over time are *longitudinal data* (sometimes called *panel data*), which follows the same individuals (the "panel") for months, years, or sometimes decades; and *time-series data*—any data collected at relatively regular intervals over an extended period of time. The major macroeconomic indicators—such as gross domestic product and the monthly unemployment rate—are time-series data, since they have been reported monthly or annually for many decades. Daily stock prices for a group of companies are also time-series data. Certain ongoing surveys and public opinion polls intentionally ask the same question in the same way over many years, which creates a time series of public opinion on certain topics. Longitudinal data is relatively rare, although several longitudinal data sets are mentioned in chapter 20. Time-series data on a variety of topics is readily available.

Unit of Analysis and Unit of Observation

In the context of data reference, the distinction between *unit of analysis* and *unit of observation* is subtle but important. The unit of analysis is the type or level of thing that the patron wishes to study. For example, in an education study, plausible units of analysis could be students, teachers, schools, school districts, states, or countries. The unit of observation, on the other hand, is the type or level of thing about which the original researchers gathered data. Different units of analysis often, but not always, require different units of observation in the data sets. For example, a researcher who wants to compare average test scores in different school districts (using school districts as the unit of analysis) would want different data than a researcher who wants to study how students' socioeconomic backgrounds affect their test scores (using students as the unit of analysis), even though both might approach the reference desk asking for "data about students' test scores." The patron who wants to compare test scores across school districts may be able to use data with individual students as the unit of observation, as long as the data file contains a school district for each student; the patron could use that data to calculate average test scores by school district. The opposite is not true: the patron who wants to use students as the unit of analysis is not likely to be satisfied by data with school districts as the unit of observation.

North American Industry Classification System Codes

North American Industry Classification System (NAICS) codes (www.census .gov/eos/www/naics/) are used by the governments of the United States, Canada, and Mexico as well as some private data sources, to classify businesses and workers into industries for statistical purposes. These codes, which range in length from two digits (designating broad sectors) to six digits (designating specific industries) are arranged hierarchically, so that adding additional digits to the end of a broader code allows one to designate a more narrowly defined industry within the sector. For example, by adding digits to 62, "Health Care and Social Assistance," one can move to 622, "Hospitals," and then to 6222 "Psychiatric and Substance Abuse Hospitals." For many industries, the most specific code is actually a five-digit code (or occasionally even a four-digit code), and the five-digit codes are the most specific codes that can reliably be used for comparisons with data disseminated by Mexico and Canada. In the cases where a five-digit code is the most specific, some data interfaces offer an identically labeled six-digit code with a "0" on the end as an option. The examples below illustrate the system, using the 2012 version of NAICS:

44–45	Retail Trade
445	Food and Beverage Stores

4452	Specialty Food Stores
44529	Other Specialty Food Stores
445291	Baked Goods Stores
51	Information
515	Broadcasting (except Internet)
5151	Radio and Television Broadcasting
51512	Television Broadcasting
515120	Television Broadcasting

Different sets of classification codes are used by the United Nations and other organizations, and also for international trade data. Although the codes differ, the basic concept of adding digits to numbers to designate more specific industries or products is incorporated into all of the systems. These systems include the Standard International Trade Classification (SITC), a product classification (e.g., "beverages," "textile yarn") that is managed by the United Nations; International Standard Industrial Classification (ISIC), an industry classification (e.g., "manufacture of beverages," "spinning, weaving and finishing of textiles") that is also managed by the United Nations; the Harmonized System (HS), a product classification that is managed by the World Customs Organization; and Schedule B, product classification managed by the U.S. Census Bureau that is based on the HS. These codes are primarily encountered in the sources listed in chapter 16.

WHO GATHERS AND DISSEMINATES DATA?

Data collection and dissemination are expensive, time-consuming enterprises. Developing and testing a survey, hiring and training interviewers, paying postage or telephone charges, following up with people who do not respond, cleaning and analyzing the data: the costs add up quickly. Plus, in many areas it is not a profitable activity for the organizations that undertake it; much of the time, the decision to gather and share data is driven by academic or administrative motives rather than profit. These two factors of data gathering and data sharing—high costs and often low pecuniary rewards—mean that in many areas governments and intergovernmental organizations with large budgets and no need to show a profit are the best or only source of data. This is especially true for data about small geographic areas, such as provinces and counties. Thousands of times more respondents are needed to be able to calculate accurate estimates for each of the three thousand-plus counties in the United States than to calculate an accurate estimate for the entire United States, for example, which makes it substantially more expensive to conduct a survey capable of producing county-level data than one intended to produce only national data.

Additionally, to get comprehensive and complete data, it is helpful to have strong incentives to cooperate with the data collection process—another area in which governments have an advantage over private organizations. For example, in the United States business executives can be fined thousands of dollars for not responding to the Economic Census or for responding with false information.[2] Private organizations that wish to survey U.S. businesses have a much harder time finding similarly effective incentives to convince businesses to cooperate with their efforts.

Both the U.S. federal government and the UN system have extensive mechanisms for gathering and disseminating data on a wide range of topics. A brief overview of both institutions' data-gathering and data-disseminating agencies follows; for complete information about what data is disseminated by each of these agencies, please see the relevant listing in chapter 2.

United States

Although dozens of agencies, bureaus, and other divisions within the U.S. government produce some data resources, thirteen are considered the major statistical agencies:

Bureau of Economic Analysis

Bureau of Justice Statistics

Bureau of Labor Statistics

Bureau of Transportation Statistics

Census Bureau

Economic Research Service of the Department of Agriculture

Energy Information Administration

National Agricultural Statistics Service

National Center for Education Statistics

National Center for Health Statistics

National Center for Science and Engineering Statistics

Office of Research, Evaluation and Statistics of the Social Security Administration

Statistics of Income Division of the Internal Revenue Service

Approximately eighty-five other agencies, from the Consumer Product Safety Commission to the Fish and Wildlife Service, also collect some data on certain topics and release it to the public.[3] These organizations cooperate and coordinate with each other in various ways, from jointly developing standards through the Federal Committee on Statistical Methodology to operating a portal, FedStats (www.fedstats.gov), with links to many of the federal government websites that contain data and statistics.

United Nations

As with the United States, in the UN system responsibility for gathering and disseminating data is spread across many separate agencies. Chief among these is the United Nations Statistics Division, which is responsible itself for gathering statistics in certain areas (including, among others, commodities, energy, and national accounts) and which also provides assistance and standards for the statistics-gathering activities of others. Other UN agencies that gather and disseminate data include the following:

Food and Agriculture Organization
International Labour Organization
International Telecommunications Union
Joint United Nations Programme on HIV/AIDS
United Nations Children's Fund
United Nations Development Programme
United Nations Educational, Social, and Cultural Organization
United Nations Framework Convention on Climate Change
United Nations High Commissioner for Refugees
United Nations Industrial Development Organization
United Nations Office on Drugs and Crime
United Nations Population Division
World Health Organization
World Meteorological Organization
World Tourism Organization

Private Data Collection and Dissemination

Although government and intergovernmental agencies are often the best sources for data, on some subjects private organizations have a distinct advantage. For example, political constraints sometimes affect the data that government agencies can gather. In the United States, it is illegal for the Census Bureau to ask questions about religious affiliation. France forbids its government agencies from collecting data about people's race or ethnicity. When restrictions such as these are in place, one must rely on nongovernmental sources for data. Also, government and intergovernmental agencies typically do not ask public opinion or polling type questions in their surveys, such as questions about whether people favor or oppose various pieces of pending legislation or how good of a job they think the president is doing. Again, for this type of data, private organizations are the best sources.

WHAT DATA IS NOT DISSEMINATED?

Not all data that is gathered is disseminated, often for reasons of cost. Calculating aggregate data and preparing microdata for public release cost money, so typically only the data that is likely to be of highest interest goes through the process that leads to public dissemination. When the microdata is released, however, patrons can often use it to calculate the aggregate data or statistics they want even if the original researchers did not calculate or disseminate those particular figures themselves. Luckily, many major surveys, including the General Social Survey (chapter 24) and the Current Population Survey (chapter 20), do disseminate much of their microdata to the public.

Even when microdata files are released to the public, as with the aforementioned surveys, data points that could compromise respondents' privacy are usually not included in these public-use data files. Although these microdata files are composed of data about specific individuals, this microdata is carefully deidentified—information that could identify individuals, such as names and street addresses, is removed—and cleaned to be sure that it is either impossible or extremely difficult to identify the specific person or business who provided each data point. This process sometimes involves removing potentially useful data from the microdata files. In particular, very old ages and very high incomes are rare and make it relatively easy to figure out who a particular individual is in a microdata file, so these are often top-coded—that is, for ages or incomes over a certain level, the file does not give the specific age or income, just an indication that it is over that level. Sometimes, but not always, data with potentially identity-revealing data such as this is available as restricted-use data, which can be accessed only by well-qualified researchers under strict conditions of use.

The suppression of data to protect respondents' privacy is a particularly important factor to consider when looking, not just for microdata, but also for data for small geographic areas. The Census Bureau and other government agencies do not release aggregate data about very small groups of people or businesses, since this data could allow someone to make accurate guesses about the characteristics of individual identifiable people or business establishments. For example, the Census Bureau conducts a survey called County

Business Patterns that provides county-level aggregate data about the number of establishments, number of paid employees, and payroll by industry. When disseminating this data, the Census Bureau suppresses information such as the number of employees and annual payroll for industries with only a handful of establishments in that county. Otherwise, if you worked at Establishment A and knew for certain how many employees you had and what you were paying them, and if your friend worked for Establishment B and knew for certain how many employees it had and what it paid them, the two of you together could use the data from County Business Patterns to make a good guess as to how many employees Establishment C has and how much it is paying them—information that Establishment C does not want to be shared with its competitors.

Administrative data is more complicated; some is released only when it has been aggregated to the point that individual cases cannot be identified, but other types are intentionally disseminated as individually identifiable microdata. For example, by U.S. law political campaigns must release the names, addresses, occupations, and employers of people who donate more than $200 to any single federal campaign. People who have been arrested or convicted of a crime may have some of their personally identifying information revealed in conjunction with that legal action. In many states, the names, job titles, and salaries of public employees are public information that can be downloaded and used as data. These examples are, however, exceptional; for most subjects of interest, individually identifiable microdata is not available.

BEGINNING YOUR DATA SEARCH

For librarians accustomed to the relatively organized world of books and journal articles, trying to find data can be a frustrating experience. There is no single WorldCat-like portal for data; there is no data-specific set of standard subject headings; and the standards for citing data in publications are weak to nonexistent, making it challenging to track down a specific data set from a secondary source. (See appendix A for more information about the problems of data citations.) As a general rule, the following progression is useful. First, try the general sources listed in chapter 2. If none of those appear likely to contain the necessary data, move on to the subject-specific data resources listed in chapters 3–26. Then, if the data still cannot be found, try the ideas in chapter 27. As you become more familiar with many of the most common data sources and the dissemination of data more generally, you may begin to find that a different method of attack works better for your personal research style and the types of questions most commonly asked by your patrons.

NOTES

1. "Data Series LNS14000000," *Bureau of Labor Statistics*, http://data.bls.gov/timeseries/LNS14000000.
2. United States Census Bureau, "2012 Economic Census FAQs," *2012 Economic Census Advance Information*, http://bhs.econ.census.gov/bhs/ecad/SUR1_1.html.
3. The current list of federal agencies that spend more than $500,000 in a year on statistical activities can be found in the annual publication *Statistical Programs of the United States Government* (www.whitehouse.gov/omb/inforeg_statpolicy#sp/).

2
General Sources

THE SOURCES COVERED IN THIS CHAPTER ARE GENERAL-PURPOSE data sources, containing information across a broad range of subject areas. All contain a mix of demographic, economic, and social data; some also have data on additional topics. In some cases, these are the definitive sources for the fields they cover; in others, they are useful for "one-stop shopping," but more detailed data is available from a more specific source covered in a later chapter.

MAJOR SOURCES: UNITED STATES

Census Bureau (U.S. Department of Commerce)

Most people are familiar with the Census Bureau and the Decennial Census as sources for basic demographic information about the United States.[1] But the Census Bureau's data offerings go far beyond basic demographic data: they are also one of the best sources for many types of economic information about the United States—which makes more sense when you remember that the Census Bureau is a division of the Department of Commerce. The Census

Bureau runs many ongoing surveys of businesses, including the Economic Census, County Business Patterns, and the Annual Survey of Manufactures. In collaboration with the Bureau of Labor Statistics it manages the Current Population Survey, which provides the raw data for U.S. labor force statistics such as the unemployment rate. It is a major source of data on governments as employers and financial actors through products such as the Annual Survey of State and Local Government Finances; and of data on imports into and exports out of the United States. These economic surveys are covered in more depth in chapters 9 and 16, respectively.

Data from the Census Bureau is available in a variety of ways, but the most useful option for many purposes is American FactFinder (http://factfinder2.census.gov). American FactFinder provides several options for navigating many of the Census Bureau's data sets, from the simple—browsing by geographic area or being walked step-by-step through a guided search—to power search options appropriate for advanced users. One drawback of American FactFinder is that it is focused on current data; no data from before 2000 is available. The most comprehensive and easy-to-use source for historical data from the U.S. Census Bureau is the National Historical Geographic Information System, a nongovernmental project discussed below.

For more than one hundred years before the launch of American FactFinder, the *Statistical Abstract of the United States* was the go-to source for statistics about the United States. In this print volume, the Census Bureau brought together hundreds of tables on just about every conceivable subject—from the number of people who participate in various sporting activities to the amount of hazardous waste generated in each state—produced using its own data, data from other government agencies, and, in later years, proprietary data licensed from private organizations. Then, facing budgetary constraints in 2011, the Census Bureau decided to eliminate the Statistical Compendia program, which published the *Statistical Abstract* and two similar volumes focused on subnational data, the *State and Metropolitan Area Data Book* and the *County and City Data Book*. The 2012 edition was the last version of the *Statistical Abstract* published by the Census Bureau.[2] As of this writing, the volumes of the *Statistical Abstract* published from 1878 through 2012 remained available on the Census Bureau's website (www.census.gov/compendia/statab/past_years.html).

Data.Gov (U.S. General Services Administration)

Data.gov (www.data.gov)—the official portal to data produced by the U.S. federal government—is more comprehensive than the Census Bureau's offerings, since it includes data across a broader range of subject areas. Data from all fifteen cabinet-level agencies—the departments of Agriculture, Commerce, Defense, Education, Energy, Health and Human Services, Homeland

Security, Housing and Urban Development, Interior, Justice, Labor, State, Transportation, Treasury, and Veterans Affairs—are included in its tens of thousands of available data sets, as is data from some of the many non-cabinet-level agencies, including the Federal Communications Commission, the Consumer Product Safety Commission, and the National Aeronautics and Space Administration. Data.gov also contains information about and links to data disseminated by nonfederal organizations, such as state and local government agencies. The sheer variety of types of data available is a great strength for users who know exactly what they are looking for and know how to recognize it when they see it, but it can contribute to making the site overwhelming for those less knowledgeable. Different data sets can be downloaded in different formats, from spreadsheets and PDF documents to RDF and JSON files. Additionally, a few hundred interactive datasets can be queried or manipulated online.

MAJOR SOURCES: WORLD

United Nations

The United Nations may be the single largest disseminator of freely available data from all countries in the world. Although a plethora of separate agencies within the UN system each publish data in their own domains, the United Nations brings a large portion (although nowhere near all) of these statistics together in a single, cross-searchable site, UNdata (http://data.un.org). In addition to the data collected by its own divisions, the United Nations also uses UNdata to distribute numeric information from other, independent international organizations, such as the World Bank and the International Monetary Fund.

Major agencies whose data are available, in whole or in part, through UNdata include the following:

Food and Agriculture Organization
International Labour Organization
International Monetary Fund
International Telecommunications Union
Joint United Nations Programme on HIV/AIDS
United Nations Children's Fund
United Nations Development Programme
United Nations Educational, Social, and Cultural Organization
United Nations Framework Convention on Climate Change
United Nations High Commissioner for Refugees

United Nations Industrial Development Organization
United Nations Office on Drugs and Crime
United Nations Population Division
United Nations Statistics Division
World Bank
World Health Organization
World Meteorological Organization
World Tourism Organization

Note that, for many of these organizations, only some of their data is available through UNdata; the remainder is distributed only via their own websites. Agencies with significant data resources that are not available in UNdata are covered in the relevant sections later in this book.

World Bank

Although some of the World Bank's data is available through UNdata, much of it is available only on the World Bank's own data site (http://data.worldbank.org). The World Bank's mission—to fight poverty and related problems in poor and middle-income countries—informs the data it makes available: thousands of indicators that are directly or indirectly related to the economic well-being of countries and their populations, including indicators of macroeconomic performance, economic inequality, the labor market, the health and education of the population, government spending, environmental quality, and gender discrimination in employment and education. More than eight thousand of these indicators are available in online interfaces that allow for visualizing the data on maps or in graphs, viewing data in tables, or downloading data sets.

MINOR SOURCES

National Historical Geographic Information System
(University of Minnesota)

The National Historical Geographic Information System (NHGIS, www.nhgis.org), a project of the Minnesota Population Center at the University of Minnesota, distributes an impressive quantity of historical data originally collected by the U.S. Census Bureau. This includes not only population data from the Decennial Census and American Community Survey but also data from County Business Patterns, the censuses of churches and other religious bodies conducted between 1906 and 1952, agricultural data from various sources covering 1840–1959, and various special censuses conducted in the

1920s and 1930s. The data is compatible with GIS software but can also be opened and manipulated as spreadsheets.

European Union

The Eurostat database (http://ec.europa.eu/eurostat) provides access to harmonized, nation-level data for countries that are currently part of or are candidates for joining the European Union. The database contains statistics related to a wide variety of topics, including agriculture, trade, labor, health, education, and other economic and socioeconomic topics. Free registration is required for access to some data sets and download formats. More advanced users can also access Eurostat data through the European Union Open Data Portal (http://open-data.europa.eu/en/), which provides access to the data in Linked Data and other specialized formats.

Organisation for Economic Co-operation and Development

Another source for general data on European countries, as well as for other developed and upper-middle-income countries, is OECD.StatExtracts (http://stats.oecd.org), produced by the Organisation for Economic Co-operation and Development (OECD). This database includes only so-called core data from the OECD; additional data can be accessed through OECD's subscription product, iLibrary. The data that is freely available is broad and deep, covering topics ranging from productivity to pesticides, tax revenues to tobacco use, and immigration to technological innovation. The length of time series available varies, but some data is available as far back as the 1940s or 1950s. (To access additional years of historical data, where available, open the "Customize" menu and choose "Time & Frequency" under the "Selection" options.)

Regional Economic and Social Commissions and Regional Development Banks

Two types of regional sources, the United Nations Regional Economic and Social Commissions and the regional development banks, can be helpful for patrons who need data about multiple countries in the same geographic region. All of these organizations have an interest in some aspect of economic and social development in their region, and the data they disseminate broadly reflects this interest. (The possible exception is the United Nations Economic Commission for Europe, whose membership consists almost entirely of developed countries and which focuses instead on economic integration.) They all produce economic data, but because they are concerned with development broadly defined many of them also publish social, political, and in some cases even environmental data for their respective regions. Development banks and regional economic commissions that make significant data resources freely available on their websites include the following:

African Development Bank Group (AFDB, http://dataportal.afdb.org/Default.aspx). The AFDB's Data Portal offers a variety of methods for accessing dozens of economic and social indicators for African countries: maps, "dashboards" that display related charts on a single screen, a "data analysis" option that allows users to manipulate data as they could in a desktop spreadsheet program, and traditional static spreadsheets.

Asian Development Bank (www.adb.org/statistics/). Of the approximately 750 indicators available in its Statistical Database System, over half are purely economic and financial, covering such topics as government finance, inflation, and trade, and the remaining indicators primarily cover social and socioeconomic issues. Statistics are also available in a variety of PDF publications.

Inter-American Development Bank (IDB, www.iadb.org). IDB makes available a variety of separate databases and downloadable data sets, from the purely economic (e.g., REVELA, which reports on expectations for inflation and economic growth) to the largely social (e.g., Sociómetro-BID, which contains copious data about the education, housing, and other indicators of socioeconomic status of countries' populations, broken down by gender, race, and other demographic factors). IDB also has an entire database of indicators of the quality of a country's governance, DataGov (see chapter 23).

United Nations Economic Commission for Africa (UNECA, www.uneca.org). UNECA's statistical system, variously called the ECA Databank or StatBase (http://ecastats.uneca.org/statbase/), has data on trade, agriculture, and other economic variables; on health, education, and other social variables; and on the environment, among other topics. Several indicators are listed, but many of them are not available for every country for every year. Note that the site seems not to work in Firefox, although it works in most other browsers.

United Nations Economic Commission for Europe (UNECE, www.unece.org). The UNECE Statistical Database contains data in six areas: economics, forestry, gender, transportation, the Millennium Development Goals, and international migration.

United Nations Economic Commission for Latin America and the Caribbean (ECLAC in English, CEPAL in Spanish, www.eclac.cl). ECLAC's statistical database, CEPALSTAT/Databases and Statistical Publications, has a user-friendly interface, with data presented in charts and graphs for basic users, in interactive interfaces with download options for intermediate users, and via an application programming interface for the most advanced users. It also provides extensive data on the environment, sustainability, and social cohesion, in addition to the standard economic and social indicators. Be aware, though, that it is possible to stumble into partially untranslated areas in CEPALSTAT, so some knowledge of Spanish can be helpful.

United Nations Economic and Social Commission for Asia and the Pacific (UN ESCAP, www.unescap.org). ESCAP's statistical database includes many common economic, financial, and socioeconomic indicators, but it is notable for the breadth of data on environmental issues. Many indicators are available covering such topics as emissions of carbon dioxide and other pollutants, water usage, and protections for endangered species. Health and education data are also well covered by this database.

A fifth regional commission, the Economic and Social Commission for Western Asia (www.escwa.un.org), does not publish a statistical database, but some statistical information can be found in PDFs on its website.

National Statistical Agencies

One of the most useful single web pages for general statistical information seeking is "Statistics—National Agencies and Compendia" (www.library.vanderbilt.edu/govdb/natlstats.html), published by the Jean and Alexander Heard Library at Vanderbilt University. It contains links to the local equivalent of the Census Bureau and the Statistical Abstract, where available, for every country in the world, as well as notes about the languages in which information is available. If statistics are needed for a single country, and those statistics are not readily available in one of the other sources mentioned in this book, searching the data produced by the country's national statistical agency is an excellent next step in one's data search.

Open Knowledge Foundation

The Open Knowledge Foundation (http://okfn.org), a not-for-profit group based in Cambridge, England, is responsible for multiple wide-ranging catalogs of freely available data sets. These include datacatalogues.org, a "catalog of catalogs" with links to more than three hundred sites containing open data, and PublicData.eu, which contains almost 20,000 data sets for countries in Europe. Because of the international nature of the Open Knowledge Foundation sites, some of the data may be available only with non-English-language metadata.

Gapminder

No discussion of general data sources would be complete without mentioning the Gapminder site (www.gapminder.org). Gapminder is notable not primarily for its data—Gapminder merely disseminates data that is widely available from other sources, although the breadth of the data it has assembled is impressive—but for the interactive interface it puts over the data. This interface has been made famous by Hans Rosling's 2006 TED talk. (If you have 20 minutes and you haven't seen the video yet, it is well worth your time.)[3] Gapminder's interface allows users to visualize data in five dimensions at once (*x* axis, *y* axis, bubble size, color, and time). Time is fixed, but for all other dimensions users can choose which variables they want to be represented. The interface makes visualization so easy that users may not even realize how much data they are taking in at once.

Following the success of the Gapminder interface, similar moving "bubble charts" or "motion charts" have become available on other sites, including those of the United Nations Development Programme (UNDP, http://hdr.undp.org/en/data/explorer/), which can be used to explore the data that goes into the UNDP's Human Development Reports (indicators covering social and economic issues, health, education, the environment, and technology); and the Google Public Data Explorer (www.google.com/publicdata/directory/), which allows users to visualize data from various U.S. and international agencies.

NOTES

1. Until 2010, the Decennial Census (the every-ten-year undertaking commonly referred to in the United States as "the Census") itself was a rich source of data about the employment, education, and income of American individuals, households, and families; one household in six received the so-called long form, with dozens of questions about everything from the amount of rent they paid on their residence and whether they had moved in the past five years to how well each person spoke English and how much schooling he or she had completed. After the 2000 Census, all questions beyond the most basic demographics (age, gender, race, and Hispanic ethnicity), plus one additional question (whether the residence was rented, owned free and clear, or owned but with outstanding loans), were dropped from the Decennial Census and moved to a new survey, the American Community Survey, which is covered in chapter 20.
2. ProQuest began publishing its own version of the *Statistical Abstract* in print and as an online subscription starting with the 2013 edition.
3. Hans Rosling, "The Best Stats You've Ever Seen," Feb. 2006, www.ted.com/talks/hans_rosling_shows_the_best_stats_you_ve_ever_seen.html.

3
Agriculture and Food

THE SOURCES IN THIS CHAPTER COVER AGRICULTURE BROADLY defined, including not just growing crops and raising animals for food but also forestry, fishing, and other activities that involve harvesting living things for economic purposes. In addition to production, the consumption of food is covered by some of the listed sources.

MAJOR SOURCES: UNITED STATES

Economic Research Service
(U.S. Department of Agriculture)
National Agricultural Statistics Service
(U.S. Department of Agriculture)

The U.S. Department of Agriculture (USDA) is, along with the Department of Commerce, one of only two cabinet-level departments that contain two major federal statistical agencies. Collectively, these two agencies, the Economic

Research Service of the USDA (ERS, www.ers.usda.gov) and the National Agricultural Statistics Service (NASS, www.nass.usda.gov), provide much of the easily available agricultural data for the United States.

The boundary between data one should expect to find through the ERS and through NASS is often fuzzy. In general, NASS is more concerned with data about agricultural production (e.g., number of acres devoted to growing specific crops, cost of renting or buying farmland, amounts of pesticides and fertilizers used by farmers, prices farmers receive for their crops), whereas the ERS is more concerned with data about agricultural and food policy (e.g., agricultural productivity rates, quality of life and federal spending in rural areas, prices consumers pay for their groceries). However, the ERS disseminates, and in some cases does additional analyses of, data collected by many other statistical agencies, including the Census Bureau and NASS, when that data relates to agriculture, food, or rural life.

The ERS is also a good source for data about the foods that Americans eat.[1] Through its Food Availability (per Capita) Data System, the ERS provides detailed, time-series information on the availability of various types of food, from chili peppers to flour, often going back several decades—as far as 1909 for some major commodities, including milk, beef, pork, and sugar. Because the USDA manages the Supplemental Nutrition Assistance Program (SNAP, colloquially known as "food stamps"), county-level time-series data about the number of people receiving food assistance benefits and the dollar value of those benefits is available through the ERS as well.

NASS is responsible for the Census of Agriculture, an every-five-year survey covering every farm in the United States, as well as a bevy of smaller, often more frequent surveys covering everything from catfish farms to Christmas tree production. If it can be grown or raised in the United States, NASS probably has at least some data about its production. A full list of topics covered in NASS surveys is available on the NASS website (www.nass.usda.gov/Surveys/index.asp), along with links to the relevant surveys. The frequency of these surveys varies. Some are monthly (e.g., Agricultural Yield Survey, Chickens and Eggs Survey) or annual (Organic Production Survey). Others are less frequent: every three years (e.g., Nursery and Christmas Tree Survey, Nursery and Floriculture Chemical Use Survey), every five years (On-Farm Energy Production Survey), or even every ten years (Census of Horticultural Specialties). County-level and ZIP code–level data from the Census of Agriculture about agricultural production, the demographics of farmers, and farm income is available on the NASS site, as are links to reports containing data from the other NASS surveys.

MAJOR SOURCES: WORLD

Food and Agriculture Organization (United Nations)

Internationally, the United Nations Food and Agriculture Organization (FAO) is the major source for statistics on agriculture and food. FAO's definition of agriculture is broad, encompassing forestry, fisheries, and water and soil conditions affecting agriculture as well as growing crops.

Most FAO data is in the FAOSTAT database (http://faostat3.fao.org), which covers the production of and international trade in crops, livestock, and wood products; producer prices for a variety of crops; measures of the amount of food and nutrients available to the population of a given country; spending on agricultural machinery and other capital investments; use of fertilizers and pesticides; and related topics. The interface is conveniently divided into sections for different types of users; selecting the options to browse or compare data automatically takes users into a highly graphical interface that provides data highlights, primarily in chart and graph form; selecting the options to search or download data allows advanced users to download data in spreadsheet form for further analysis.

Another database, the GIEWS Food Price Data and Analysis Tool (www.fao.org/giews/pricetool/), provides monthly time-series data on the prices of specific food items in specific cities, primarily in developing countries. Data is available from 1990 to present, although there is more data for more recent years. The food items vary by country, depending on the cuisine of the area; the prices of rice, wheat, and maize are reported for many areas, but the price of chickpeas is reported only for cities in Ethiopia, Eritrea, and India and for the country of Tunisia, for example.

The FAO also maintains separate databases with information on specific aspects of food and agriculture, such as livestock production, fisheries, and water resources. Many of these databases can be accessed via the "Statistics" page on the FAO site. Databases with detailed information about land use and soil conditions are listed on the "Databases/Information Systems" page in the "Land Resources" section of the site. Much of the data accessed via the latter list is geospatial data designed for GIS use.

MINOR SOURCES

World Food Programme

Another UN agency with a stake in data about food availability is the World Food Programme, which distributes food aid to areas threatened with famine in the wake of disasters or wars. Its Food Aid Information System (www.wfp.org/fais/) reports data from 1988 to present on the types and quantities of international food aid provided to various countries, the donors (countries or international organizations) who provided the food aid, and the nutritional value of that aid.

International Food Policy Research Institute

The International Food Policy Research Institute (IFPRI, www.ifpri.org), headquartered in Washington, DC, has been publishing research into policies that can help fight hunger and malnutrition since 1975. After completing a free registration, users can access all of the data sets used in IFPRI's published research. These include both household-level surveys covering families' food consumption, finances, and additional topics as well as macroeconomic data sets, including "social accounting matrices" for many countries. These social accounting matrices include data on the flow of money and commodities, particularly agricultural commodities, through a nation's economy.

OECD.StatExtracts

(Organisation for Economic Co-operation and Development)

Eurostat

(European Union)

The general statistics databases for the OECD and European Union both contain information about agriculture in their member countries and beyond. In OECD.StatExtracts (covered more fully in chapter 2), that data includes estimates of the amount and type of agricultural and food-related subsidies provided directly to farmers, to consumers, and to support agriculture in the country generally, in both OECD and non-OECD countries. The EU's Eurostat database (see chapter 2), which contains data on EU member countries only, includes data on the number, size, and type of farms per country; the amount of crops and livestock produced and land farmed organically; the amount of fish wild-caught in the oceans and seas near Europe and the amount farm-raised; and statistics about fishing fleets; farming-related environmental indicators such as pesticide, herbicide, fungicide, and fertilizer use and the extent of irrigation; land-use data; forestry statistics; and data on many other agriculture-related topics.

United Nations Economic Commission for Europe Statistical Database

The United Nations Economic Commission for Europe (http://w3.unece.org/pxweb/) database has detailed data for several dozen European forestry-related variables, typically beginning in 1990 and reported every five years.

Available data sets include the number of square hectares of forest, the number of square hectares of forest damaged by forces ranging from storms to insect infestations, various measures of the biological diversity of the forests, and various measures of the economic benefits of forests, from the amount of wood harvested to the number of people employed in manufacturing wood and paper products. Data is available by country, by forest or "other wooded land," and, for some variables, by forest type (e.g., alpine forest, broadleaved evergreen forest, floodplain forest).

UnctadStat

(United Nations Conference on Trade and Development)

The United Nations Conference on Trade and Development (UNCTAD) maintains price data on agricultural commodities in its UnctadStat database (http://unctadstat.unctad.org, "Commodities" tab). This data has a longer time series than the data in the GIEWS Food Price Data and Analysis Tool (discussed above), covering 1960 to present for some commodities and some countries.

NOTE

1. Another good source of data about the foods Americans eat is the National Health and Nutrition Examination Survey, covered in chapter 19.

4
Crime

THIS CHAPTER COVERS COMMON CRIMES, THEIR VICTIMS, AND the criminals who commit them. International and politically motivated crimes are not covered here, except to the extent that, for example, a politically motivated assassination would be counted as a murder in the murder statistics. Sources for data about both domestic and international terrorism are listed in chapter 22; some sources for data about human rights violations and other such international crimes are also listed in that chapter. Additionally, a small amount of data about political corruption is available from some of the sources listed in chapters 21 and 23.

For the purposes of this book, substance abuse is considered to be primarily a health issue, not a crime issue. Data on drug arrests is available from some of the sources covered in this chapter, but data on drug use generally in the United States is available from the Substance Abuse and Mental Health Services Administration and from the National Institute on Drug Abuse, both covered in chapter 19.

MAJOR SOURCES: UNITED STATES

Bureau of Justice Statistics (U.S. Department of Justice)
Federal Bureau of Investigation (U.S. Department of Justice)

The Bureau of Justice Statistics (BJS) and the Federal Bureau of Investigation (FBI), both contained within the Department of Justice, provide similar data—the number of crimes committed in the United States—collected through very different methods. The BJS (www.bjs.gov) gathers much of its crime data via the National Crime Victimization Survey, which interviews approximately 75,000 teenagers and adults annually about a wide range of crimes—including nonviolent crimes such as identity theft—committed against themselves or their property. The Uniform Crime Reports from the FBI, in contrast, are compiled from administrative records: local police departments provide information to the FBI about the crimes reported to each department. Data from the Uniform Crime Reports is available in online publications on the FBI site (www.fbi.gov/about-us/cjis/ucr/), most notably the long-running annual series *Crime in the United States*, and in a separate interactive database (www.ucrdatatool.gov).

The advantages of the National Crime Victimization Survey are that it captures crimes that are not reported to the police (which are a majority of crimes), and that it includes many more types of crime than the Uniform Crime Reports, which cover only homicide, rape, aggravated assault, robbery, burglary, theft, and arson.[1] The advantages of the Uniform Crime Reports are that they offer a longer time series: Uniform Crime Reports have been published since 1930 and have data online back to 1960, whereas the National Crime Victimization Survey began in 1973. They also allow for more geographic detail; data from the Uniform Crime Reports is available for geographic areas as small as cities, whereas the National Crime Victimization Survey typically provides only national estimates. Also, only Uniform Crime Reports can be used for statistics on homicides; as the BJS site drily notes, "Murder is not measured by the NCVS because of an inability to question the victim."

In addition to the National Crime Victimization Survey, the BJS also runs a variety of censuses and surveys of persons and institutions involved in the criminal justice system: the Annual Survey of Jails, the Census of Public Defender Offices, the National Computer Security Survey, the Survey of Law Enforcement Gang Units, and many more. A full list of BJS data collection programs is available via the "Data Collections" tab of the BJS website.

MAJOR SOURCES: WORLD

United Nations Office on Drugs and Crime

The United Nations Office on Drugs and Crime (UNODC) is the major source for internationally comparable crime data. Only some of its data (basic homicide statistics) is available on data.un.org; most is distributed through its own site (www.unodc.org, "Data and analysis" tab). The data goes back to 1970 but is patchy, with many countries not reporting for every year. The focus is on violent crime, drug use, and theft and burglary; there is also data on the number of people detained, prosecuted, and convicted for any crime.

MINOR SOURCES

U.S. Border Patrol (U.S. Department of Homeland Security)

In the United States, crimes related to international borders—such as persons attempting to enter the country without the appropriate documentation, or attempts to smuggle drugs and other illegal goods—are handled by the U.S. Border Patrol. It releases its own statistics for apprehensions and seizures of people and goods related to crimes such as these (www.cbp.gov/xp/cgov/border_security/, "U.S. Border Patrol" tab). Beware the confusing introductory page, which makes it appear as if statistics are available for only a few recent fiscal years. The dates given are the years in which the reports were published, not the years they cover. Historical reports with long time series—at least one as far back as 1960—are available to users if they click through and examine the titles of the reports published each year.

International Crime Victimization Survey

Although the data from the International Crime Victimization Survey (ICVS, http://web2012.unicri.it/services/library_documentation/publications/icvs/) is now somewhat dated—the surveys were conducted between 1989 and 2005—it is still one of the richest sources of internationally comparable data on crime. The survey produced statistics on the rates at which people were victims of certain crimes, including robbery, burglary, various types of thefts, consumer fraud, and sexual assaults. Information was also gathered on whether the crime was reported to the police, and the reason why not if it was not reported, as well as on people's opinions of the police, their personal safety, and their likelihood of being victimized by crimes. The European Crime and Safety Survey (EU ICS), a related project, asked similar questions. Microdata from both projects from 1989 to 2005 are available via Data Archiving and Networked Services (DANS, www.dans.knaw.nl) after free registration. The microdata from ICVS from 1989 to 2000 is freely available on the ICVS site without registration.

Local Jurisdictions

Crime is one of the subject areas in which microdata is more likely to be readily available. Many jurisdictions release data on individual crimes reported in that area (although not all of this data is available online in an easily usable format), and, for several cities, private websites collect this data and make it available in a user-friendly interface. An interactive map posted by the *Philadelphia Inquirer* is one good example of such an interface.[2] On a larger scale, CrimeMapping.com, created by the Omega Group (a company that sells products that allow police departments to analyze crime data geographically), displays crime data from well over one hundred municipalities nationwide, including large cities such as Detroit, Los Angeles, and Miami.

Internationally, the United Kingdom illustrates what can be done when crime data is released in an easily usable format. Several official sites—including Police.uk (www.police.uk), which covers the entire country, and the Metropolitan Police website (www.met.police.uk/crimefigures/), which covers London—provide interactive mapping interfaces for a range of crime data. Police.uk provides information not only about reported crimes but about the resolution of those cases, and it also makes it easy for users to download the raw data behind the maps. Several private groups have created their own interfaces to that data; links to those interfaces can be found at www.police.uk/apps?q=.

National Archive of Criminal Justice Data

Another source for microdata related to crime and criminal justice is the National Archive of Criminal Justice Data (www.icpsr.umich.edu/icpsrweb/NACJD/). This site is hosted by the Interuniversity Consortium for Political and Social Research (ICPSR), a major microdata archive at the University of Michigan. It distributes microdata from several government agencies with an interest in crime, including the BJS, the Office of Juvenile Justice and Delinquency Prevention (www.ojjdp.gov), and the National Institute of Justice (www.nij.gov), as well as some nongovernmental data. Although the vast majority of the two-thousand-plus data sets are from the United States, a few are international. Some of the data sets in the NACJD can be analyzed online using SDA (see appendix B). Most of this data is freely available after registering, but a few of the nongovernmental data sets are available only to users at institutions with ICPSR subscriptions.

NOTES

1. According to data from the 2006–2010 National Crime Victimization Surveys, 58 percent of crimes are not reported to the police; *Victimizations Not Reported to the Police, 2006–2010,* U.S. Department of Justice, 2012, http://bjs.ojp.usdoj.gov/content/pub/pdf/vnrp0610.pdf.
2. "Homicides in Philadelphia," *Philadelphia Inquirer,* www.philly.com/philly/news/special_packages/inquirer/Philadelphia_Homicides_1988_2011.html.

5
Earth Science—General

THIS CHAPTER INCLUDES SOURCES FOR EARTH SCIENCE DATA generally as well as sources for specific aspects of earth science not covered elsewhere in this book—namely, natural hazards, geology, soil science, and biogeography (the geographic distribution of biological organisms). Most atmospheric data, including most data on air pollution, is in chapter 6, although some atmospheric data can be found in the general-purpose earth science databases covered in this chapter as well. Data on climate, including indicators of climate change (e.g., data on receding glaciers or greenhouse gas emissions), is also covered in chapter 6. Data about hydrology, as well as some oceanographic data, is reviewed in chapter 7. Some additional sources for data about soil conditions as they relate to farming are in chapter 3.

MAJOR SOURCES: UNITED STATES

U.S. Geological Survey (U.S. Department of the Interior)

The U.S. Geological Survey (USGS) disseminates massive quantities of data about several aspects of earth science, both data generated by its own activities and data created by other organizations. This data is available through several different portals:

Analyses of the amounts of various chemicals found in the soil, in rocks, in water, and in stream sediments for tens of thousands of locations in the United States are available in the "Geochemistry" section of the "Mineral Resources On-Line Spatial Data" site (http://mrdata.usgs.gov). Other data sets disseminated through this site include the locations and other information about different types of mineral deposits, mines, and copper smelters in the United States and around the world as well as mining claims made on land owned by the U.S. government.

Data on volcanic activity can be accessed via the site of the Volcano Hazards Program (http://volcanoes.usgs.gov), which contains links to each of the five separate volcano observatories that gather data about volcanos in the United States—one each for Alaska, California, the Cascades, Hawaii, and Yellowstone. In some cases the most complete data is available only via each volcano's respective observatory, not on the main Volcano Hazards Program site.

Data on the time, location, depth, and magnitude of earthquakes around the world can be found via the Earthquake Hazards Program (http://earthquake.usgs.gov). The comprehensive, searchable data in the ANSS Comprehensive Earthquake Catalog, also known as ComCat, is available 1900 to present. Large data files with information on the likelihood of various earthquake hazards at different locations in the United States are also available, as is detailed data on the estimated number of casualties from various hazards (shaking, landslides, tsunamis) generated by more than 22,000 earthquakes beginning in 1900.

The National Gap Analysis Program's site (http://gapanalysis.usgs.gov) distributes data on land cover (the type of vegetation or manmade structures on a given piece of land), the areas where it is believed that various types of animals live, and protected land areas, with the goal of helping scientists and the general public protect important animal habitats. Data is also available for some aquatic habitats, such as lakes and river basins.

Thousands of USGS data sets can be found by searching Data.gov, the federal data catalog (see chapter 2).

Additional USGS data is available through both the EarthExplorer site (http://earthexplorer.usgs.gov; free registration required to download data), which provides access to data sets derived from aerial photography and satellite-based instruments, and The National Map (http://nationalmap.gov), which has spatial data sets with information on land cover, natural hazards such as floods and wildfires, conservation status, and a few other topics. Since the data available through EarthExplorer and The National Map is primarily spatial, these sites are covered more fully in chapter 26.

National Aeronautics and Space Administration

The National Aeronautics and Space Administration (NASA) is one of the major providers of information about the earth via its Earth Observing System and associated Earth Observing System Data and Information System (EOSDIS). Through EOSDIS, NASA gathers and disseminates a wide range of data on all aspects of earth science—everything from sea ice to monsoons and from land cover to ocean color.

EOSDIS data holdings are dividing among several separate data centers and "distributed active archive centers"—some of which are managed by organizations other than NASA—but the data held by these centers can be cross-searched using the Reverb tool (http://reverb.echo.nasa.gov/reverb/). Reverb offers several highly user-friendly search options, including the ability to draw a bounding box on a digital map and see all data sets available for that area. Other options include searching by a single date range or by specific months, days, and times in any year (e.g., data from the month of January, or from 9:00 a.m. on June 21, regardless of the year). Sophisticated users can even upload a shapefile (a type of file used in GIS software) and search for data contained in an area defined by that file.

Alternately, the data held by each EOSDIS center can be searched individually on the center's own website. Many of the data centers have specialized interfaces to their data that allow users to visualize or otherwise manipulate the data they hold, an appealing feature for users who know which data center has the information they need. A full list of the centers and of the specific data tools they make available to the public is available on the EOSDIS website.

EOSDIS data can also be searched via the Global Change Master Directory (see chapter 6).

Environmental Protection Agency

Data on topics such as hazardous waste, air and water quality, and the release of toxic chemicals into the environment is available from the Environmental Protection Agency (EPA), by way of two major entry points. The Data Finder (www.epa.gov/datafinder/) contains links to EPA data sources organized by topic (drinking water contaminants, hazardous waste, etc.) The databases are generally not cross-searchable in this interface, so it is most helpful for users who want bulk data on a single topic. The other interface, Envirofacts (www.epa.gov/enviro/index.html), is more useful for patrons seeking data on a wide range of environmental topics for a specific geographic area or type of facility. It allows users to generate a list of facilities meeting certain criteria—for example, in a certain state or ZIP code, on or near a certain tribal area, in a certain line of business, or releasing a certain pollutant—and to view or download data on those facilities from many different EPA systems, including the Toxics Release Inventory (through which data is reported on the emissions of various chemicals from industrial plants and other facilities) and the Facility Registry System (which contains basic information about facilities, e.g., the owners of the facilities and their primary activities as indicated by their NAICS codes). Users can also look up facilities by name, if they know the specific facility in which they are interested. Data on public drinking water systems is also available through Envirofacts.

MAJOR SOURCES: WORLD

Institute for Environment and Sustainability

(European Commission)

The Institute for Environment and Sustainability (IES, http://ies.jrc.ec.europa.eu/index.php), part of the Joint Research Centre operated by the European Commission, maintains more than a dozen data portals providing access to several different types of scientific data. These include the European Soil Portal, which, despite its name, also contains some data for soils in areas outside of Europe; the European Drought Observatory, the Floods Portal, and the European Forest Fire Information System (EFFIS), all of which contain both current and several decades of historical data on droughts, floods, and forest fires in Europe as well as data about risks for these events; the European Alien Species Information Network (EASIN), which distributes data on the number and geographic distribution of invasive species in Europe; and the European Forest Data Centre (EFDAC), which provides access to, among others, data sets on the current and possible future locations where various tree species are likely to grow given climate change forecasts. Several more IES portals are covered in other chapters where they are most relevant.

European Environment Agency

The European Environment Agency, part of the European Union, distributes several dozen data sets about environmental issues in the countries of Europe (www.eea.europa.eu/data-and-maps/data/). These include data sets about land cover as well as species distributions, habitats, and protected areas. The

Agency also distributes data concerning air quality, air pollution, and water, which are covered in chapters 6 and 7.

MINOR SOURCES

Global Land Cover Facility (University of Maryland)

Another option for accessing some satellite data is the Global Land Cover Facility (GLCF, http://glcf.umd.edu/data/) at the University of Maryland. This site provides access both to raw data from some NASA satellites (including Landsat, ASTER, and MODIS) and to data sets based on this data. These include data sets that use data from MODIS to identify areas where deforestation is occurring or vegetation is being burned (the MODIS Vegetative Cover Conversion) and that use Landsat data to create high-resolution, global estimates of the percentage of land covered by trees (Landsat Tree Cover Continuous Fields), for example. GLCF also makes available data related to the extent of natural disasters, such as Hurricanes Katrina and Rita and the earthquake that struck China in May 2008.

European Space Agency

Like NASA, the European Space Agency (ESA, www.esa.int/ESA/) has a major earth observation program that uses satellites to gather data. Access to much of this data is restricted to various degrees (some data sets require only registration and a description of the project for which the data will be used; others require that the project be approved before data access is granted), but a few projects based on ESA data are freely available with no restrictions or registration requirements. These include the ATSR World Fire Atlas (http://due.esrin.esa.int/wfa/), which provides data on the locations of fires worldwide, 1995 to present; Culture-MERIS (http://due.esrin.esa.int/culturemeris/), which uses the Normalized Difference Vegetation Index (NDVI) to provide information on the density of vegetation; and GlobCover (http://due.esrin.esa.int/globcover/), which provides data on land cover.

ISRIC—World Soil Information

ISRIC—World Soil Information (www.isric.org, formerly International Soil Reference and Information Centre) is an international organization that provides data sets related to soil types and soil degradation. These include both data sets covering the entire world and others that are country-specific. One of the global data sets, "World Soil Profiles," is a crowdsourced effort to gather and harmonize as many historic soil profiles as possible. ISRIC data is also available through the Global Change Master Directory (see chapter 6).

6

Earth Science—Air, Climate, and Weather

THE SOURCES IN THIS CHAPTER PROVIDE METEOROLOGICAL and climatological data—that is, data on weather (i.e., short-term events) and climate (long-term patterns), including indicators of climate change. Data on air pollution is also covered, although other forms of pollution are addressed in chapters 5 and 7. Sources that contain climatological or meteorological data along with data on other earth science disciplines also appear in chapter 5. Most of the data on the emission of greenhouse gases is covered in this chapter, but there is additional information on gases from burning certain fuels in chapter 18.

MAJOR SOURCES: UNITED STATES

National Oceanic and Atmospheric Administration

The National Oceanic and Atmospheric Administration (NOAA) is the primary source for data on climate and weather in the United States, and it also disseminates a large amount of data for the rest of the world. This data—which includes everything from numeric data recorded by thousands of weather stations worldwide, to archived radar data, to historical climate data based on tree rings—is distributed through a variety of sites, but the most comprehensive selection is available through Climate.gov (www.climate.gov). This site allows users to perform a keyword search on, or to browse through, approximately three hundred climate-related and weather-related data sets produced or distributed by NOAA. The date ranges vary for different geographic areas and types of data, but some land-based weather observation data is available for the nineteenth century, and ship-based observations for some ocean areas can even be found for the seventeenth and eighteenth centuries.

The most user-friendly way to find data on Climate.gov may be the map applications. Some of these applications allow users to visualize the data online, but all of them allow users to choose locations, typically by drawing shapes on a map, and to download data for the locations within that area. For several of the maps, a "simplified" data access option allows for easy downloading, or one can choose the "advanced" access option for more control over variables.

Unfortunately, for many of the maps, once a user has selected locations he or she is sent to a legacy NOAA site to complete the download process, and the interfaces for these legacy sites are not always as user-friendly as they could be. In some cases data cannot be downloaded directly from the site; users have to select the data they want and enter their e-mail address, and the site then e-mails them a link to download their selected data. Data formats vary; any particular data set may be available as human-friendly PDFs, spreadsheet-friendly CSV files, or plain-text ASCII files, among other possible formats.

One particular strength of Climate.gov is its wide range of paleoclimatic data—data about the climate of the distant past. This includes data gathered from ice cores, fossilized plankton, and lake sediments, to name just a few examples. Many of these data sets can be downloaded in KML format, which allows them to be explored in Google Earth, and bulk downloads via FTP are also available for many data sets. Data produced by various climate models is also available.

Environmental Protection Agency

The Environmental Protection Agency Data Finder (www.epa.gov/datafinder/) is the primary gateway to data on air pollution, as well as other forms of pollution, in the United States. Since the EPA considers carbon dioxide and other greenhouse gases to be a form of air pollution, it also gathers and disseminates data on the emission of those gases.

The EPA releases data through various tools and portals, some intended for broad audiences and some for sophisticated researchers who need very raw data. One good example of this is the Air Quality System (AQS), which contains hourly or daily data about the level of several different air pollutants at hundreds of locations, 1980 to present. Data from AQS is available through three different interfaces. Raw data on dozens of air pollutants can be accessed via the AQS Data Mart (www.epa.gov/ttn/airs/aqsdatamart/access.htm), although users must e-mail the EPA and request access to the system. Less advanced users will likely prefer to access the data via AirData (www.epa.gov/airdata/), which allows options such as viewing summary statistics and creating tile plots, time-series plots, and animated maps showing the levels of six primary air pollutants at selected locations in the United States. Another user-friendly access point to the AQS data is the AirCompare site (www.epa.gov/aircompare/), which allows users to compare the air quality of different counties or states, or at different times of year, in up to ten counties.

Two EPA programs disseminate data on the pollutants released by individual plants or other facilities, with one focusing specifically on greenhouse gases and the other providing data for air pollution more broadly. The former, the Facility Level Information on Greenhouse Gases Tool (FLIGHT, http://ghgdata.epa.gov/ghgp/main.do), allows users to browse information about the metric tons of carbon dioxide, methane, nitrous oxide, and various fluorinated gases released by thousands of individual plants or other facilities that are major emitters of these gases. Bulk downloads of this data are also available. The latter, the Air Facility System Search (AFS, www.epa.gov/enviro/facts/afs/search.html), allows users to search for facilities within a given geographic area and to view information about those facilities' compliance with regulations governing the release of air pollutants.

Comprehensive data on the emission of air pollutants is published every three years as part of the National Emissions Inventory (NEI, www.epa.gov/ttn/chief/eiinformation.html). Like the systems discussed in the previous paragraph, this data set contains "point data" on individual facilities that release air pollutants, but it also includes estimates for what is called "nonpoint data"—sources of air pollution that are not inventoried by current reporting and compliance programs, such as the pollution released by the furnaces in individual homes. The data set also contains estimates of the air pollutants released by "mobile sources," such as airplanes, farm machinery, and motor vehicles. Data can be downloaded at the national, state, county, or tribal area level and is also available broken down by sources, such as "wildfires," "dry cleaning," or "locomotives."

National Aeronautics and Space Administration

The National Aeronautics and Space Administration (NASA) facilitates access to a great deal of data on climate change through its Global Change Master Directory (GCMD, http://gcmd.gsfc.nasa.gov). This site brings together metadata from thousands of data sets from dozens of research projects, including both research done by NASA itself and research by other scientists, international organizations, foreign government agencies, and other organizations. Several discovery methods are provided: users can keyword search across the whole collection, browse by topic across the whole collection, draw bounding boxes on a map and find all data pertaining to areas contained in the box, or enter separate portals organized by data providers and research projects. The types of data covered range broadly, including topics from paleoclimates and atmospheric chemistry to solar activity and fungi. The site is, however, a data directory, not a database; users must follow links to the sites of the organizations that produced the data sets in order to access them.

MAJOR SOURCES: WORLD

World Meteorological Organization

The World Meteorological Organization (WMO), which is part of the UN system, publishes "standard normals" for various climate indicators. These measures typically represent an average for one of three thirty-year periods—1901–1930, 1931–1960, and 1961–1990—although in some cases other time periods were used. Some of these standard normals, such as the monthly maximum and minimum air temperature, have been computed for hundreds of locations in more than one hundred countries, but in other cases data has been produced only for a much shorter list of locations. The 1961–1990 data is most readily available; it is disseminated both through the UNdata site (see chapter 3) and through Climate.gov (discussed above). Additional WMO data, including daily weather observations for thousands of stations around the world, can also be accessed through the map applications or the bulk data downloads on Climate.gov.

Carbon Dioxide Information Analysis Center

Although the Carbon Dioxide Information Analysis Center (CDIAC, http://cdiac.ornl.gov) is a U.S. government agency (in the U.S. Department of Energy), it is one of the major global sources for data about the emission of greenhouse gases. CDIAC hosts the World Data Center for Atmospheric Trace Gases, and its data on carbon dioxide emissions is one of the official indicators used by the United Nations to monitor progress toward the Millennium Development Goals related to environmental sustainability (and thus some CDIAC data on carbon dioxide emissions can be found in the many databases that include the Millennium Development Goals indicators, such as UNdata). CDIAC provides access to dozens of data sets related to carbon dioxide and climate change. In addition to the previously mentioned data on carbon dioxide emissions, its website also allows users to find and access information such as concentrations of carbon dioxide in the atmosphere both presently and historically; historical estimates of carbon dioxide emissions back to 1751; carbon stored in biomass and soils; and historical weather and climate indicators such as temperature, precipitation, and clouds. In addition to data on carbon dioxide, some data on ozone, methane, chlorofluorocarbons, carbon monoxide, and other gases is available.

MINOR SOURCES

United Nations Framework Convention on Climate Change

The United Nations Framework Convention on Climate Change (UNFCCC, http://unfccc.int/ghg_data/items/3800.php) gathers data on the emission of various greenhouse gases, 1990 to present. Unlike the CDIAC carbon dioxide emissions data, which contains annual estimates for more than two hundred countries and territories, the UNFCCC has comprehensive annual data only for the forty-two countries that are parties to Annex I of the Climate Change Convention, plus Kazakhstan. For many other countries, information is available for some years. All of the data is self-reported by the individual countries.

Emissions Database for Global Atmospheric Research

(European Commission)

The Emissions Database for Global Atmospheric Research (EDGAR, http://edgar.jrc.ec.europa.eu/index.php), one of several Joint Research Centres sponsored by the European Commission, provides estimates of the emissions of several different types of harmful gases, including greenhouse gases (e.g., carbon dioxide, methane, and several different fluorinated gases), particulate matter, and gases that contribute to acid rain (e.g., sulfur dioxide and nitrogen oxides). Data is available by country or economic sector, or in a gridded format, with emissions per 0.1 degree by 0.1 degree cell. Several different data sets cover different time periods with different degrees of precision; the oldest estimates go back to 1890, whereas the most detailed data is available only for recent years.

European Environment Agency

The European Environment Agency, part of the European Union, distributes data sets about a wide range of environmental issues in the countries of

Europe (www.eea.europa.eu/data-and-maps/data). These include several useful, detailed data sets about air quality and emissions. One data set contains plant-level data on emissions of sulfur dioxide, nitrogen oxides, and particulates ("dust") for thousands of plants in twenty-seven European countries. Another, AirBase, contains air quality data for thousands of locations across the continent. There are also country-level data sets on emission of air pollutants.

7
Earth Science—Water

THE SOURCES IN THIS CHAPTER PROVIDE DATA ON ALL FORMS of water: surface waters such as rivers and lakes, groundwater, and oceans. The primary focus is on data about water quality, such as chemical contaminants or algae blooms, although several of the sources also provide more general data on water.

MAJOR SOURCES: UNITED STATES

U.S. Geological Survey (U.S. Department of the Interior)

Hydrological data from the U.S. Geological Survey (USGS) is available from the National Water Information System (http://waterdata.usgs.gov), which distributes data collected from more than one million streams, wells, and other sites in the United States. The depth of water in the stream, river, or other body of water is available for many locations, as is data on the groundwater level for wells; data on the volume of water flowing through streams is also widely available. Some sites also report such information as temperature and turbidity of the water and level of various chemicals in the water, as well as meteorological data for the location. Data is automatically recorded one to four times per hour, then transmitted to the USGS every few hours, so up-to-date information is available through the site. This raw data is available for 2007 to present; daily, monthly, and annual summaries are available for a much longer time period, with some sites going back to the early nineteenth century.

Environmental Protection Agency

Two Environmental Protection Agency data sets that deal specifically with water quality are STORET (www.epa.gov/storet/dbtop.html) and Watershed Assessment, Tracking and Environmental Results (WATERS, http://water.epa.gov/scitech/datait/tools/waters/index.cfm). STORET gathers and disseminates the results of water quality assessments collected by various government and nongovernmental agencies. Different types of water quality assessments are available, including not only chemical analyses of water itself but analyses of contaminants in fish living in that water, data about the plants, animals and microbes living in the water, and more. WATERS provides data about waters that are considered to be impaired because of problems such as algae overgrowth, pollutants such as mercury or PCBs, or microbes such as E. coli.

There are several different ways to access data from these two systems. One, the Surf Your Watershed tool (http://cfpub.epa.gov/surf/locate/index.cfm), allows users to identify quickly the watersheds in a given geographic area, access the STORET monitoring data gathered in a selected watershed, and view the WATERS water quality assessment report, which contains data on the amount of water (miles of streams and rivers, or acres of reservoirs and lakes) and the specific bodies of water in a selected watershed that are considered to be impaired for each reason. Another, the MyWATERS Mapper (http://watersgeo.epa.gov/mwm/), allows users to browse, visualize, and download water quality data on an interactive map. Data from WATERS is also available in GIS-compatible formats (http://water.epa.gov/scitech/datait/tools/waters/).

MAJOR SOURCES: WORLD

UN-Water (United Nations)

UN-Water was formed in 1993 by the United Nations to coordinate water-related activities carried out by the organizations within the UN system. Its website (www.unwater.org) provides quick access to freshwater-related data disseminated by several UN agencies, including the Food and Agriculture Organization's AQUASTAT database (www.fao.org/nr/water/aquastat/main/index.stm), which contains information about water resources and irrigation;

and the World Health Organization/United Nations Children's Fund Joint Monitoring Program for Water Supply and Sanitation (www.wssinfo.org), which tracks the number of people worldwide who do and do not have access to improved drinking water and sanitation facilities. In addition to linking to other sources for data, UN-Water also maintains a collection of water-related statistics on its own site as well as an interactive Key Water Indicators Portal (www.unwater.org/statistics_KWIP.html) that allows users to visualize eight water indicators on a map.

Water Information System for Europe

The Water Information System for Europe (WISE, http://water.europa.eu) is a joint project of four European agencies. WISE data resources are contained on the sites of two of these agencies. Eurostat, the general statistical agency of the European Union (see chapter 2), provides national and subnational data on water usage, water resources, and wastewater treatment. More data is available from the European Environment Agency (www.eea.europa.eu/themes/water/dc), which disseminates data sets primarily focused on measures of water quality, on releases of various chemicals into water, and on wastewater treatment. GIS files of water-related data, including locations of rivers and their watersheds, are also available from the European Environment Agency.

MINOR SOURCES

National Oceanic and Atmospheric Administration
(U.S. Department of Commerce)

Most of the National Oceanic and Atmospheric Administration (NOAA) data source are covered in chapter 6, but its oceanographic data sets deserve a separate mention here. Thousands of NOAA data sets covering topics such as water temperature, salinity, oxygen levels, water depth, and algal blooms are available both through Data.gov (the overarching U.S. government data portal, covered in chapter 2) and through the website of NOAA's National Oceanographic Data Center (www.nodc.noaa.gov/index.html). Date ranges for the different types of data vary widely, but some information is available as far back as 1773.

Institute for Environment and Sustainability
(European Commission)

The Institute for Environment and Sustainability (IES) maintains two portals with oceanographic data: the Environmental Marine Information System

(EMIS, http://emis.jrc.ec.europa.eu), which focuses on the waters surrounding the European continent, and the Global Marine Information System (GMIS, http://gmis.jrc.ec.europa.eu), which covers the entire world. Both sites have an interactive mapping interface that allows users not only to visualize the data but also to perform some online analyses of it. Similar data is provided through these two sites, although a few more variables and a greater resolution are available in EMIS. Both sites have time-series data, with time series of several decades available for some variables.

8
Economics—General

THIS AND THE NEXT SEVERAL CHAPTERS PROVIDE SOURCES for economic data. This chapter focuses on general sources for economic data, that is, sources with a wide-ranging interest in many aspects of the functioning of the economy. Because these sources tend to take a broad view of the economy, they are typically best for macroeconomic data such as gross domestic product, employment and unemployment rates, and rates of inflation; note, however, that the most detailed data sources specifically for macroeconomic accounts are in chapter 13. Subsequent chapters cover sources that collect and disseminate specific types of economic data, such as data on firms, commodities, or trade. Users interested in microeconomic data are more likely to find a useful source in one of these subsequent chapters.

MAJOR SOURCES: UNITED STATES

FRED (Federal Reserve Bank of St. Louis)

One of the most comprehensive economic data sources, bringing together data from multiple federal agencies as well as from private and international sources, is produced by the Federal Reserve Bank of St. Louis. This database is universally known as FRED, short for Federal Reserve Economic Data (http://research.stlouisfed.org/fred2/). FRED contains time-series data sets, typically including data up to the previous year or quarter. Much of the data, including components of the Consumer Price Index, per-capita personal income, and unemployment statistics, are available for small geographic areas. With a total of 72,000 time series available, some with one hundred years or more of data, and easy downloading to Excel, FRED is never a bad place to start when looking for economic data for the United States.

MAJOR SOURCES: WORLD

Many of the best sources for global economic data are also good general data sources. The international organizations with an interest in economic issues, such as the World Bank and the various regional UN Economic and Social Commissions, also have an interest in development more generally. Thus, they also gather and disseminate data on health, education, and many other topics beyond the purely economic. Because of this, many of the general sources listed in chapter 2 are good bets for international macroeconomic data. The following databases, which are covered in more depth in chapter 2, are some of the best places to start:

UNdata (http://data.un.org). This site contains economic data on a wide range of topics from various sources, including gross domestic product (GDP) and related indicators from the National Accounts Official Country Data produced by the United Nations Statistics Division (UNSD), financial data from the International Monetary Fund's International Financial Statistics database, manufacturing data from the INDSTAT database produced by the United Nations Industrial Development Organization, and trade data from the UNSD's Commodity Trade Statistics Database, among others.

World Bank Data (http://data.worldbank.org). This site includes data on poverty, income distribution, public finance, countries' financial sectors, and countries' business climates.

Inter-American Development Bank. The IDB maintains the Latin American and Caribbean Macro Watch Data Tool (www.iadb.org/Research/LatinMacroWatch/lmw.cfm), which contains well over one hundred common macroeconomic indicators for twenty-six countries. Most are time series with data from 1990 to present.

Asian Development Bank. The ADB publishes time series for several hundred macroeconomic indicators, 1988 to present, for its forty-eight member states in its Statistical Database System (https://sdbs.adb.org/sdbs/index.jsp).

Eurostat (http://epp.eurostat.ec.europa.eu/portal/page/portal/eurostat/home). This site provides several hundred macroeconomic indicators for members of and membership candidates for the European Union. Some of the time series are long, with some data available as far back as the late 1940s.

MINOR SOURCES

ALFRED (Federal Reserve Bank of St. Louis)
FRASER (Federal Reserve Bank of St. Louis)

In addition to FRED, the Federal Reserve Bank of St. Louis produces two databases that can be invaluable to patrons with an interest in economic history: ALFRED (Archival Federal Reserve Economic Data, http://alfred.stlouisfed.org) and FRASER (Federal Reserve Archival System for Economic Research, http://fraser.stlouisfed.org). ALFRED is useful for patrons who want to replicate previous economic analyses. It lets the user choose a date in history—as far back as 1927 for some data series—and download a data set as it existed on that date, ignoring any subsequent revisions of the data. This service is available for more than 65,000 data series. FRASER contains PDFs of government publications related in some way to the economy, dating from the founding of the U.S. Department of the Treasury in 1789. Some of these PDFs contain useful statistics and tables that are not otherwise readily available online, although, of course, to analyze the data one must first type it into a spreadsheet or other software.

Real-Time Data Research Center
(Federal Reserve Bank of Philadelphia)

The Federal Reserve Bank of St. Louis is not the only such bank to produce useful data resources. The Federal Reserve Bank of Philadelphia publishes several data sets in its Real-Time Data Research Center (www.philadelphiafed.org/research-and-data/real-time-center/), which contains up-to-date data about the state of the economy and professional economists' predictions about the direction of the economy. Data sets in the former category include the Aruoba-Diebold-Scotti Business Conditions Index, which provides a relative measure of the strength of the economy. Examples of the latter category include the semiannual Livingston Survey and the quarterly Survey of Professional Forecasters. Historical data about the past predictions used in creating certain official Federal Reserve reports, namely, the Semiannual Monetary Policy Report to the Congress and the Greenbook, are also available.

Other Federal Reserve Banks

All of the Federal Reserve Banks (in addition to the ones listed above, Boston, New York, Cleveland, Richmond, Atlanta, Chicago, Minneapolis, Kansas City, Dallas, and San Francisco) gather and disseminate data about the economies of their regions. Although the specific data gathered varies by region, common types of data include monthly surveys of manufacturers or other businesses in the region and state-level indices of economic indicators. A map of the regions, with links to all Federal Reserve Bank websites, is available at http://federalreserveeducation.org.

9
Economics—Government Finance

ONE WOULD THINK THAT DATA ABOUT GOVERNMENT FINANCE—the revenue raised and money spent by governments—would be easily accessible, since most democratic governments are, at least in theory, relatively transparent about such matters. Unfortunately, this is not always the case, especially for standardized, harmonized data. Data for the United States and its subdivisions is freely and easily available, as is data for much of Europe, but good international sources for this data are generally subscription-only.

MAJOR SOURCES: UNITED STATES

Census Bureau (U.S. Department of Commerce)

The U.S. Census Bureau maintains a "Federal, State, & Local Governments" section that disseminates data about tax revenues and expenditures for state and local governments and employment by federal, state, and local governments, including local public school districts (www.census.gov/govs/). Data is generally available online from 1992 to present from the Census Bureau site.

The Census Bureau conducts a variety of government surveys, including the Census of Governments (conducted in years ending in "2" and "7" and covering all state and local governments in the United States, including school districts), the Annual Survey of State Government Finances (www.census.gov/govs/state/), and the Annual Survey of State and Local Government Finances (www.census.gov/govs/local/). Although the specific questions vary slightly across these surveys, in general the governments are asked to provide information on the revenue they take in from various sources (e.g., collecting income or property taxes, selling school lunches, charging highway tolls, selling alcohol at state-owned liquor stores), their expenditures of various types (capital vs. operating expenses) and for various purposes (e.g., corrections, libraries, parks and recreation), their short-term and long-term debt, and their assets.

Other, specialized surveys include the following:

Annual Survey of Public Employment and Payroll (www.census.gov/govs/apes/). This survey collects data on number of full-time and part-time employees, hours worked by part-time employees, and total payroll for full-time and part-time employees by all types of government agencies, including local school districts and public universities.

Quarterly Survey of Public Pensions (www.census.gov/govs/qpr/). This survey asks the hundred largest public pension systems for financial information such as amount of money they have in various types of investments (corporate stocks, corporate bonds, etc.), amount the government contributed on behalf of its employees, amount employees contributed themselves, and amount paid out of the system.

Annual Survey of Public Pensions (www.census.gov/govs/retire/). This survey has two major differences from the Quarterly Survey: it covers almost two thousand public pension systems, and it includes questions about the number of members in each system.

USAspending (U.S. Office of Management and Budget)

Other than employment data, the Census Bureau no longer tracks data about government finance at the federal level.[1] Microdata about government spending, 2000 to present, is available from the USAspending site (www.usaspending.gov), which is run by the U.S. Office of Management and Budget. This site provides access to individual contracts, grants, and other ways in which the federal government provides money to corporations, not-for-profit organizations, and state and local government agencies. Information includes amount of spending, name and address of recipient, federal agency in charge of the spending, specific project and program for which money was spent, and dates of spending. Bulk data, with limited filtering options, can be downloaded from the "Data Feeds" page, or users can choose one of two advanced search options to find spending data based on specific criteria and use the "Export" option to download it in a CSV file. Browsing options are also available.

Some data about federal revenues, as well as aggregate information about federal spending, can be found in the historical tables of each year's Budget of the United States Government, which is published on the website of the Office of Management and Budget (www.whitehouse.gov/omb/budget/historicals/). These tables contain actual historical information on such topics as amount of revenue from personal versus corporate income taxes; spending in more than one hundred specific areas, from housing assistance to the space program; and size of the federal debt. The data series generally start somewhere between the 1930s and the 1970s, but one table—containing overall revenue, expenses, and deficit/surplus—contains data all the way from 1789. Most tables also contain projections for several years into the future.

MAJOR SOURCES: WORLD

International Monetary Fund

Unfortunately, the definitive source for internationally comparable government finance data—the International Monetary Fund's (IMF) Government Finance Statistics (GFS)—is subscription-only.[2] A limited amount of data is available for free on the IMF website (http://elibrary-data.imf.org/, under "Build your own Query"), including total government revenue, total government spending, gross government debt, and net government lending or borrowing.

Eurostat (European Commission)

For Europe, the Eurostat database contains detailed data about revenues, expenditures, and so forth of European Union countries.[3] Some of the available data is quite specific: for example, additional data options for the "general government expenditure by function" database view include "recreational and sporting services," "pollution abatement," and "street lighting." Users can also select additional historical years of data, going back to 1969 for some countries.

MINOR SOURCES

Open Knowledge Foundation

Unofficial government spending data for many countries is available from OpenSpending (http://openspending.org), a project of the Open Knowledge Foundation (OKFN, http://okfn.org). This project uses volunteers to clean up and standardize government spending data sets before uploading them to the OpenSpending platform. Once they are available on the website, anyone can visualize them as interactive treemaps or download them for more sophisticated analysis.

NOTES

1. Previously, the Census Bureau released information about federal government spending in the Consolidated Federal Funds Report (CFFR), but funding to produce this report was eliminated in the 2012 federal budget. As of this writing, historical data from the CFFR and its predecessors was still available via FTP from the Census Bureau (www2.census.gov/pub/outgoing/govs/special60/). CFFR data from 1983–2010 is available, and some other data on the site is available as far back as 1902.
2. This data is also included in the Interuniversity Consortium for Political and Social Research (ICPSR), so users at institutions that subscribe to ICPSR can access it even if they do not subscribe to the IMF's online products.
3. From the Eurostat Statistics portal (http://epp.eurostat.ec.europa.eu/portal/page/portal/government_finance_statistics/introduction), select the Database tab on the left, choose one of the few default categories, or click the indicated icon to select from many detailed categories.

10
Economics—Firms and Industries

BUSINESS-RELATED MICRODATA—DATA SUCH AS THE NET profits or the balance sheets of individual businesses—is one of the most difficult types of data to access for free. The data is voluminous—there are millions of businesses in the United States alone—and, unlike much data, business data is commercially valuable; stock traders, financial analysts, and others are willing to pay a great deal of money for data that can help them improve their earnings or beat their competitors. Aggregate data about industries, on the other hand, is much easier to access. The sources in this chapter cover both microdata on individual firms, where available, and aggregate data covering entire industries.

MAJOR SOURCES: UNITED STATES

EDGAR (U.S. Securities and Exchange Commission)

For data on specific companies, EDGAR (Electronic Data Gathering, Analysis, and Retrieval, www.sec.gov/edgar/searchedgar/webusers.htm) is the best free source for data on publicly traded companies in the United States. All such companies are required to file periodic reports with the Securities and Exchange Commission, the U.S. federal agency that operates EDGAR. These reports contain legally mandated disclosures on many topics, such as revenues, cash flows, profits or losses, and executive compensation. EDGAR is relatively easy to navigate if one is looking for data on only a few companies and knows the legal names or ticker symbols of the companies of interest. However, its options for finding companies based on criteria other than name (e.g., based on net revenues or other financial characteristics) are limited; only geography and Standard Industrial Classification (SIC) code are supported for this type of search.

Census Bureau (U.S. Department of Commerce)

On industries in general, the U.S. Census Bureau manages several surveys, some listed below, that provide detailed data on specific industries in the United States. The aggregate data from these surveys is released based on NAICS codes, a system for organizing businesses into sectors and industries that is explained in chapter 1; it may be helpful to read that explanation before attempting to access data from these sources.

Economic Census (information about the Economic Census, www.census.gov/econ/census/; access to the data, http://factfinder2.census.gov). This census contacts every "employer establishment" in the United States every five years, in the years ending in "2" or "7." An "establishment" is a single location of a business, so, for example, each individual restaurant in a chain is a separate establishment. Since the Economic Census covers only employer establishments, establishments with no employees (e.g., a plumber or caterer who runs her own business and has no assistants, or a single freelance writer) are not included.[1] The specific questions asked vary by industry, but generally each business is asked to provide detailed information about the specific type of work it carries out (e.g., if the business is part of the book publishing industry, is it a university press, an atlas or map publisher, a sheet music publisher) as well as its revenues, expenses, inventories, payroll, and number of employees.

Annual Services Report (www.census.gov/services/index.html), **Annual Retail Trade Report** (www.census.gov/retail/), and **Annual Wholesale Trade Report** (www.census.gov/wholesale/). All of these reports provide survey data on sales or revenues, inventories, and expenses for specific industries (down to six-digit NAICS codes). Some data is also available monthly (for retail and wholesale trade) or quarterly (for services).

Annual Survey of Manufactures (www.census.gov/manufacturing/asm). This survey provides more detailed information than the three aforementioned annual sector surveys. For each of hundreds of industries, from the broad (e.g., "apparel manufacturing") to the narrow (e.g., "guided missile and space vehicle propulsion unit and propulsion unit parts manufacturing"), it provides approximately seventy variables related to payroll and other labor costs, capital expenditures, other expenses, revenues, value of items shipped, and inventories. This data is available in American FactFinder (see chapter 2), 2002 to present.

County Business Patterns and **ZIP Code Business Patterns** (www.census.gov/econ/cbp/). These programs provide information about the number of establishments, number of employees, and payroll by industry for small geographic areas. Data is also available aggregated for larger geographic areas, such as metropolitan statistical areas and states. The total number of establishments in each industry (down to six-digit NAICS codes) is reported for all geographies, as is the number of establishments in each of nine size categories based on the number of employees. Payroll data and the specific number of employees are reported at the county level and higher, but only if releasing that data does not threaten to reveal the number of employees or payroll information for a specific establishment (see chapter 1 for an explanation of why data is sometimes suppressed to protect the confidentiality of specific individuals or establishments.)

Survey of Business Owners (SBO, www.census.gov/econ/sbo/). Aggregate data from this survey is available in American FactFinder (see chapter 2), but, unlike most of the Census Bureau's economic surveys, the SBO also makes microdata freely available to the public on its website (www.census.gov/econ/sbo/pums.html). It is also one of the few Census Bureau economic surveys that includes the self-employed, although it excludes farmers and a few other small industries. The SBO is particularly useful for data about businesses owned by women, racial or ethnic minorities, and military veterans, but it can also be used for data on topics such as the amount of startup capital small businesses require, reasons small businesses close, and characteristics of family-owned firms.

All of these sources provide data at the national level; many also provide state and local data. In some instances, including the Economic Census and ZIP Code Business Patterns, data is available for areas as small as ZIP codes.

These are only a few of the many economic surveys managed by the Census Bureau. The following web pages contain tables listing all of the surveys with data on a given sector as well as information about what topics are covered and what level of geographic detail is available:

- Manufacturing (www.census.gov/econ/manufacturing.html)
- Retail (www.census.gov/econ/retail.html)
- Wholesale (www.census.gov/econ/wholesale.html)
- Service Industries (www.census.gov/econ/services.html)
- Construction (www.census.gov/econ/construction.html)

MAJOR SOURCES: WORLD

Microdata for firms is one of the few areas of data reference where the freely available resources are often completely inadequate. This is especially true for users who need long historical time series, which are not available from the sources listed below. The *ALA Guide to Economics and Business Reference* (American Library Association, 2011) provides an overview of the subscription sources that provide access to this data. For libraries that do not have access to these subscription databases, the sources listed below provide short time series for some of the most commonly requested data on individual publicly traded firms.

Yahoo! Finance

Yahoo! Finance (http://finance.yahoo.com) is one useful free source for information about individual firms, especially their historical stock prices and trading volumes. Twenty years or more of stock information is freely available, in CSV format or in interactive graphs, for many stocks both domestic and international. Additional data, such as income and cash flow, is also available, but only for recent time periods. The site also provides direct links to American companies' Securities and Exchange Commission filings, but beware: these links go to EDGAR Online (www.edgar-online.com), a private subscription service, not the free EDGAR system run by the SEC (discussed above).

Financial Times

The website of the *Financial Times* newspaper (http://markets.ft.com) offers information similar to that at Yahoo, but with different time ranges. The *Financial Times* has much shorter time series for stock prices, but it provides additional years of financial data (income statement, balance sheet, and cash flow). Yahoo typically gives three years of such data for all companies; the *Financial Times* gives five years if users complete a free registration (unregistered users can view only three years). Additionally, the *Financial Times* site offers a sophisticated "stock screener" tool that allows users to identify all stocks meeting specified criteria, including country or region, sector or industry, market capitalization, and price to earnings ratio. More than 39,000 companies' stocks are included in the database.

Structural Analysis Database

(Organisation for Economic Co-operation and Development)

At the industry level, the Organisation for Economic Co-operation and Development (OECD) publishes detailed data as part of its Structural Analysis

Database (STAN, www.oecd.org/industry/ind/stanstructuralanalysisdatabase .htm), which is available through its StatExtracts system (http://stats.oecd .org). The OECD uses the International Standard Industrial Classification (ISIC), a United Nations–sponsored system which, similar to NAICS in North America, organizes businesses into sectors and industries. ISIC is not, however, as specific as NAICS; to take one example, whereas NAICS subdivides its "Construction of Buildings" categories into several smaller categories, covering new single-family housing construction, new multifamily housing construction, industrial building construction, and more, ISIC lumps all of these activities together in an undivided category for "Construction of Buildings." Data available through STAN includes measures of production, value added, intermediate inputs, operating surplus, number of employees, hours worked, labor cost, exports and imports, and capital stock, formation, and consumption. Unfortunately, data is available for only fifteen of the thirty-four members of the OECD: Austria, Belgium, the Czech Republic, Denmark, Finland, France, Germany, Hungary, Italy, Korea, the Netherlands, Norway, Slovenia, Sweden, and the United States.

National Statistical Agencies

For some OECD members whose data is not reported in STAN, the data is available from the country's own statistical bureau. Examples include Japan, where the Ministry of Economy, Trade and Industry disseminates spreadsheets and PDFs with sector-level data from its statistical website (www.meti.go.jp/ english/statistics/); the United Kingdom, where detailed data is available from the UK National Statistics Publication Hub (www.statistics.gov.uk/ hub/business-energy/index.html); Australia, where the Australian Bureau of Statistics provides data by industry group and subgroup (www.abs.gov .au, "Topics @ a Glance" tab); and New Zealand, where similarly organized data is published by Statistics New Zealand (www.stats.govt.nz, "Browse for stats" tab). Industry-level or sector-level data is also available in English from some developing countries, including Brazil (www.ibge.gov.br/english/), India (http://mospi.nic.in/Mospi_New/site/home.aspx), and China (www.stats .gov.cn/english/statisticaldata/; note that some parts of this site work only in Internet Explorer).

MINOR SOURCES

Internal Revenue Service

In the United States, the Internal Revenue Service uses its administrative records to compile certain sector-level statistics at the level of firms, which provide a slightly different perspective from the data released by the Census

Bureau for establishments. These include data such as the number of businesses filing tax returns, receipts, net income, various types of expenses and other deductions, deficit, assets, and liabilities by the sector, industry, and organizational form of the business (corporation, sole proprietorship, etc.). This data is published as part of the Statistics of Income program (www.irs.gov/uac/Tax-Stats-2), which also publishes statistics on the income of individuals.

Not-for-Profit Sector

Although not-for-profit establishments are included in the Census Bureau's economic data, they generally are not broken out as a separate category. For example, the data on not-for-profit hospitals and for-profit hospitals is usually all reported together under the industry "General medical and surgical hospitals." There are, however, a few exceptions: the Annual Services Report (discussed above), for example, separates the revenue data for many industries into establishments that are exempt from federal income tax (i.e., not-for-profit organizations) and establishments that are subject to federal income tax (i.e., for-profit businesses). The IRS, in Statistics of Income, also publishes separate tables of data for tax-exempt organizations (link from www.irs.gov/uac/Tax-Stats-2).

There are freely accessible private sources with detailed information about individual not-for-profit organizations. Two of the most useful are Charity Navigator (www.charitynavigator.org) and the Foundation Center (http://foundationcenter.org), both of which provide access to the Form 990s filed with the IRS by not-for-profit organizations. These forms include annual data about each not-for-profit's finances, including amount and sources of its revenue, expenses in various categories, assets and liabilities, total amount spent on salaries, and individual salaries of certain high-level or highly paid persons. Unfortunately, the data is available only as PDF copies of the forms, so the data must be copied out to a spreadsheet before it can be analyzed. Individual charities may also make copies of their Form 990s, or other financial information, available on their own websites for more years than are available through these sources.

NOTE

1. Data about nonemployer establishments is available in Nonemployer Statistics (www.census.gov/econ/nonemployer/), and nonemployer establishments are also included in the Survey of Business Owners.

11 Economics—Commodities

THE TERM *COMMODITIES* IS USED IN THIS CHAPTER IN ITS broad sense, to refer generally to tangible goods of all sorts that are bought and sold, rather than the narrower sense of raw agricultural products and mineral resources in which it is sometimes used. In fact, those two particular types of commodities, by and large, are not covered in this chapter: most data sources on agricultural commodities are covered in chapter 3, and data for petroleum, coal, and other fossil fuels is primarily found in chapter 18.

MAJOR SOURCES: UNITED STATES

Manufacturers' Shipments, Inventories, and Orders

(U.S. Census Bureau)

The Census Bureau publishes Manufacturers' Shipments, Inventories, and Orders (sometimes called "M3," www.census.gov/manufacturing/m3/), a monthly survey that provides data on the value of new orders, unfilled orders, shipments, and inventories from manufacturers in the United States. Data from this survey is available online from 1958 to present, so it is an excellent time series. However, the data is not particularly granular; only eighty-nine categories are available for this survey, ranging from "Apparel" and "Household Appliances" to "Ships and Boats" and "Construction Machinery."

Annual Survey of Manufactures (U.S. Census Bureau)

The Annual Survey of Manufactures (www.census.gov/manufacturing/asm/, see chapter 10) is another source for data on the production of goods in the United States. The data is available only annually, and it includes only the values of shipments, but it covers hundreds of granular categories—not just household appliances, for example, but specifically cooking appliances, refrigerators and home freezers, laundry equipment, and so on.

Current Industrial Reports (U.S. Census Bureau)

Prior to 2011, Current Industrial Reports (www.census.gov/manufacturing/cir/index.html), a project of the U.S. Census Bureau, published granular data on the production of various commodities, from flour to electrocardiograph machines, on a monthly, quarterly, or annual basis. It even had sixteen separate categories for socks, specifying whether the socks were for men, women, or infants and whether they were cotton, wool, manmade materials, or other materials. This program was discontinued because of budget constraints; the final data releases cover through July 2011. Only data for 2010 and the first half of 2011 are available on the Census Bureau's website, but older data can be obtained in print at some federal depository libraries.

MAJOR SOURCES: WORLD

Industrial Commodity Statistics Database
(United Nations Statistics Division)

The United Nations produces the Industrial Commodity Statistics Database, whose data is available via the UNdata site (http://data.un.org; see chapter 2). For around six hundred different items, from bulldozers to sunglasses, the database contains one or both of two annual measures of production: value (in U.S. dollars), and a measure of the physical quantity manufactured, such as metric tons or individual units. Data is available from 1995 to approximately four years from the current date.

UnctadStat

(United Nations Conference on Trade and Development)

Another UN product, UnctadStat (http://unctadstat.unctad.org), provides prices and price indices for agricultural products (wheat, coffee, beef, wool, etc.) and minerals (lead, tin, gold, petroleum, etc.), with a long time series for this data—1960 to present for some commodities. An index representing instability in commodity prices is also available, 1983 to present.

MINOR SOURCES

Financial Times

The *Financial Times* newspaper (http://markets.ft.com; free registration required) provides approximately five years of historical data on the prices of certain metals, fuels, and agricultural products, as well as European carbon emissions, in its "Data Archive." This data set has one major drawback: information can be downloaded only one day at a time, in PDF files, so assembling a long time series is a time-consuming process.

12 Economics—Labor

LABOR STATISTICS, SUCH AS EMPLOYMENT AND UNEMPLOYment rates and average rates of pay for workers, often cannot be cleanly separated from other technically nonlabor statistics such as data related to education and income. This is especially true in the United States, where the Bureau of Labor Statistics collaborates with the Census Bureau on several surveys that are used to generate both labor and nonlabor statistics. With one exception, this chapter discusses only data sets that are specifically and solely about labor. Data sets with a mix of labor and nonlabor statistics are included in chapter 20.

MAJOR SOURCES: UNITED STATES

Bureau of Labor Statistics (U.S. Department of Labor)

The Bureau of Labor Statistics (BLS) is the primary source of data on the labor market in the United States. It is responsible, in whole or in part, for numerous surveys and other data collection activities. Despite its name, the BLS gathers data on much more than simply the labor market; it is also a key source of data on such economic topics as inflation, consumer spending, and productivity. The BLS data that deals directly with the labor market is listed below; other categories are covered in the chapters where they are most relevant. Note also that much BLS data is available through FRED (see chapter 8).

Current Employment Statistics (CES, www.bls.gov/ces/). This survey provides monthly information about number of workers, average hours worked, and average hourly wages by industry, 1990 to present. The CES survey covers most employees, but it does not include the self-employed, farm workers, and a few other small employment categories. It is also used to generate employment estimates for states and metropolitan areas; these estimates are available on a separate website (www.bls.gov/sae/home.htm).

Quarterly Census of Employment and Wages (CEW, www.bls.gov/cew/). This census provides some data similar to that from the CES survey—number of workers and their average weekly wage by industry—but with a few important differences. The CEW contains additional data series, including number of establishments, total amount of wages paid, and average annual pay (wages or salaries). Because the CEW is a *census* (in which every employer provides information) rather than a *survey* (in which only a sample of employers are contacted), it is able to provide more detailed breakdowns of the data than the CES. The data is theoretically available for small geographic areas such as counties and metropolitan statistical areas and for specific industries—down to six-digit NAICS codes, which designate such specific industries as "boat dealers," "strawberry farming," and "bottled water manufacturing." In practice, federal disclosure policies mean that much of this data may be restricted if too narrowly focused in geography, industry, or, especially, both at once (see chapter 1, for an explanation of why information about small groups is often suppressed from data releases such as these, as well as a fuller explanation of NAICS codes).

Occupational Employment Statistics (OES, www.bls.gov/oes/). In contrast to the CES and CEW reports, which gather employment and wage data by *industry*, Occupational Employment Statistics gathers data by *occupation*. The OES provides the number of people working in an occupation, fraction of all jobs in a specific occupation (expressed as jobs per 1,000 jobs), and data about the mean and various percentile wages for hundreds of specific occupations—everything from fundraisers, tax preparers, archivists, and computer network architects to bartenders, tree trimmers, aircraft cargo handling supervisors, and dredge operators. At the national level, there are also two indicators of the distribution of occupations in specific industries: percentage of workers employed in a given industry who are in that occupation, and percentage of establishments in a given industry that employ someone in a specific occupation. This data also allows for examining differences in mean and median wages between people working in the same occupation but in different industries, such as retail sales workers in automobile dealerships versus those in furniture stores. At the state and local level, there is data about how the fraction of jobs in a specific occupation in that area compares to the fraction of jobs in that occupation nationwide, an indicator called the "location quotient."[1]

National Compensation Survey (NCS, www.bls.gov/eci/). Despite its name, the National Compensation Survey is not necessarily the best source for detailed data about wage and salary rates; products such as the CEW or OES are often better sources for this type of data, especially if data is needed for a specific occupation or geographic area.[2] Instead, the NCS aims to provide an overall measurement of employment costs, which is the amount employers must pay, on average, to retain a single employee. This includes both wages and benefits such as health insurance and pension plans. This data is released in three major series: the Employment Cost Index, which measures relative changes in wages and salaries, benefits, and total compensation (wages and salaries plus benefits) for various broad industries and occupations; Employer Costs for Employee Compensation, which provides an average dollar figure for wages and for specific benefits (vacation time, overtime, health insurance, workers' compensation payments, Social Security payments, etc.) by several business characteristics, including region of the country, metropolitan versus nonmetropolitan location, union versus nonunion business, broad type of occupation, broad industry, and business size (measured by number of employees); and the National Compensation Survey—Benefits (previously the Employee Benefits Survey), which contains data about workers' access to approximately forty different benefits, from paid military leave to health insurance benefits for unmarried same-sex partners.

Employment Projections (www.bls.gov/emp/). The BLS also makes predictions about what the labor force will look like ten years into the future. The most commonly cited of these predictions are about how many people will be working in various occupations and industries in the future, but the BLS also releases projections on topics such as the number and demographics of people in the labor force and the number and demographics of people entering and leaving the labor force.[3]

Local Area Unemployment Statistics (www.bls.gov/lau/). As its name suggests, this program provides basic employment/unemployment data (number of people employed, number of people in the labor force, and number and percentage of people unemployed) for subnational areas of the United States, including states, counties, regions, metropolitan and micropolitan areas, and some cities and towns (in New England, all cities and towns; in the rest of the country, only those with populations over 25,000).

Job Openings and Labor Turnover Survey (www.bls.gov/jlt/). This survey provides monthly data by broad industry for six indicators of turnover, 2000 to present. The indicators are job openings, people hired, total number of people who left jobs, and three types of separations: people who quit, people who were laid off, and people who left their job for another reason.

Current Population Survey (www.bls.gov/cps/). The Current Population Survey and its predecessors have been surveying Americans about their employment status since 1940, although the various online interfaces to the data typically offer access only back to the 1960s, at best. The modern Current Population Survey continues to be used to generate unemployment and labor force statistics, but it has also expanded to include many other topics, both employment-related and socioeconomic (education, income, etc.). Because of the breadth of the survey, the CPS is of interest to many researchers, not just labor economists. The data from this survey can be and has been used to inform many political and social debates: on the BLS site itself one can find statistics about number of working mothers, number of people not employed because of poor health, number of workers who are part of a union, and number and percentage of workers in various industries who earn at or below minimum wage, for example, all generated from the Current Population Survey. The Census Bureau (which comanages this survey with the BLS) produces and disseminates additional statistics from the data. Microdata from the Current Population Survey is available from multiple sources (see chapter 20 for more information about accessing this data).

MAJOR SOURCES: WORLD

International Labour Organization

The International Labour Organization (ILO, www.ilo.org), part of the United Nations, compiles a great deal of data about workers and the labor market. For many years its major database was LABORSTA (http://laborsta.ilo.org), but LABORSTA has recently been replaced by a new database, ILOSTAT (www.ilo.org/ilostat/). Some data in ILOSTAT is available as far back as 1945 for some countries, including the size of the economically active population and the number of people working in various industries and occupations; other data, including employment and unemployment numbers and rates and the numbers and rates of occupational injuries in various industries, are available as far back as 1969, although again only for some countries. Other data with shorter time series includes average hours worked per week and average earnings in a large number of occupations, as well as data about migrant workers.

Key Indicators of the Labour Market (KILM, http://kilm.ilo.org) is another major data source from the ILO. The data is available in an interactive online interface (http://kilm.ilo.org/kilmnet/), as a PDF, and as downloadable software. The data, which spans the years 1980 to present, covers topics similar to those included in ILOSTAT—e.g., employment and unemployment rates, hours worked, wages—although there are a few variables that are included only in one of the two sources. However, whereas ILOSTAT merely disseminates data reported to the ILO by individual countries, the team that produces KILM works to harmonize the data, making it safer to attempt cross-country comparisons.

MINOR SOURCES

Census Bureau (U.S. Department of Commerce)

Although the BLS is the primary disseminator of U.S. labor statistics, a few other government agencies also release their own employment-related data. One of these is the Census Bureau, which publishes several labor-related data series. These include the Quarterly Workforce Indicators (QWI), one of the data sets contained in the Longitudinal Employer-Household Dynamics program (LEHD, http://lehd.ces.census.gov), as well as Nonemployer Statistics (www.census.gov/econ/nonemployer/).

The QWI is unusual among labor data sets in that it is longitudinal (it follows workers over a period of time) and that it is compiled from administrative data (specifically, employers' quarterly submissions to each state's unemployment insurance office) rather than from surveys or censuses. It allows for detailed breakdowns—down to counties or metropolitan statistical areas geographically; to two-digit NAICS codes by industry; and by race, age group, education, and gender of employees—for total employment, increase or decrease in number of jobs, newly created jobs, newly hired employees, employees leaving jobs, turnover, average monthly earnings, and average earnings for new hires.

The Census Bureau also provides data on self-employed workers, a group that is left out of some BLS resources for employment statistics. Nonemployer Statistics provides industry-level counts and receipts for businesses with no employees other than the owner of the business—for example, a self-employed hairdresser or a freelance graphic designer—at the national, state, county, and metropolitan and micropolitan statistical area levels. Another economically focused Census Bureau data set that includes the self-employed is the Survey of Business Owners (www.census.gov/econ/sbo/; see chapter 10).

NOTES

1. For example, in 2012 in Ann Arbor, Michigan, home of the University of Michigan, 6.24 per 1,000 jobs belonged to "English Language and Literature Teachers, Postsecondary" (i.e., English professors, or other types of English

instructors, at a college or university). The location quotient for that occupation in that location was 11.19, indicating that English professors were more than eleven times more common in the Ann Arbor workforce than in the workforce of the United States as a whole, where only 0.558 out of every 1,000 jobs belonged to English professors.

2. The NCS was once better at providing detailed data for small geographic areas and for specific jobs or industries, but one of its components, the Locality Pay Survey, was one of several statistical programs eliminated as part of federal budget cutting in 2011. Archived data from this program, 1997–2010, is still available online (www.bls.gov/ncs/ocs/).
3. State agencies use data from the BLS to make their own similar estimates for each state. These estimates are available from each state's labor agency, but they have also been gathered into a single website, Projections Central (www.projectionscentral.com).

13
Economics—Macroeconomic Accounts

Macroeconomic accounts is economics jargon for the set of statistics that describe aspects of the overall functioning of an economy. Macroeconomic accounts are often called "national accounts," but it is possible to create macroeconomic accounts for units other than nations, such as individual U.S. states or sectors of the economy. Gross domestic product (GDP) may be the most familiar macroeconomic accounts statistic, but there are many others.

MAJOR SOURCES: UNITED STATES

Bureau of Economic Analysis (U.S. Department of Commerce)

In the United States, the Bureau of Economic Analysis (www.bea.gov) is the primary source for macroeconomic accounts data. One of two major federal statistical agencies within the U.S. Department of Commerce (the other being the Census Bureau), the Bureau of Economic Analysis publishes four types of macroeconomic accounts data: national income and product accounts

(GDP; income, spending and saving by individuals; profits of corporations; value of equipment, durable goods, and other assets owned by businesses and consumers; etc.), industry accounts (inputs, output, and value-added by industry), regional accounts (GDP, personal income, and employment data, total or by industry, for states and metropolitan areas), and international accounts (imports, exports, balance of payments, etc.). Long time series are available for much of this data. Data on the amount of money invested in various categories of "fixed assets" (machinery, buildings, etc.) is available from 1901, for example, GDP is available from 1929, detailed consumer spending data is available from 1959, and much of the international accounts data is available from 1960. An interactive data interface makes it relatively easy to find, visualize, and download the data.

MAJOR SOURCES: WORLD

United Nations Statistics Division

The United Nations Statistics Division (UNSD) has a section devoted entirely to national accounts data (http://unstats.un.org/unsd/nationalaccount/). It operates the National Accounts Main Aggregates, which contains GDP, gross national income (GNI), and value-added data for both countries and the major regions of the world. Although the UNSD has been collecting and publishing national accounts data in print since the 1950s, only the data from 1970 to present is freely available in the online database.

MINOR SOURCES

Penn World Table

The Penn World Table (www.rug.nl/research/ggdc/data/penn-world-table) takes GDP, population, and exchange rate data from other sources and uses it to create purchasing-power-parity (PPP) adjusted estimates of GDP and its components for nearly all of the countries of the world, 1950 to present, with a lag of about two years. The Penn World Table was produced at the University of Pennsylvania for more than thirty years, but starting with version 8.0 it moved to new institutional hosts, the University of California–Davis and Groningen University (The Netherlands).

Maddison Project

For estimates of national accounts data before 1950, one source is the Maddison Project (www.ggdc.net/maddison/maddison-project/home.htm). The Project is named after the economic historian Angus Maddison, who spent much of his career trying to create estimates for GDP and economic growth for places and times when accurate GDP accounting was not available. The Project website distributes Maddison's data set, updated to reflect new information that has come to light since Maddison's death in 2010. It is important to be aware, when using this data, that these estimates have varying degrees of accuracy; savvy users should read the accompanying documentation for information about the sources used to create the estimates for different countries or time periods.

World Bank

Much national accounts data is also available via the World Bank (http://data.worldbank.org; see chapter 2). Although the World Bank Data site shows data only back to 1980 in the online user interface, the data downloads sometimes include additional historical data. In some instances, this can allow access to GDP and other national accounts data prior to the years made freely available online by UNSD.

14
Economics—Banks and Lending

SOME DATA ABOUT THE FINANCIAL INDUSTRY IS INCLUDED IN the sources listed in chapter 10, along with other data about the service sector. The data sets gathered about other service industries are not, however, necessarily the best types of data for understanding the conditions and activities of banks and other financial institutions. The sources in this chapter attempt to fill that gap by focusing only on the financial industry. For the United States, the sources in this chapter primarily provide microdata specifically on individual banks or individual loans. This sort of bank-level microdata is not easily available across countries; instead, the "Major Sources: World" section of this chapter provides sources for aggregate data about the banking industry and about the services it provides. The "Minor Sources" section lists a few other countries for which bank microdata is available. Note that sources for aggregate, economy-wide lending data for the United States are not included in this chapter, since that data is available through FRED (see chapter 8).

MAJOR SOURCES: UNITED STATES

Responsibility for overseeing financial institutions is dispersed across several federal agencies, in addition to the fifty states. As a result, data about financial institutions—banks, credit unions, mortgage lenders, and the like—is equally dispersed.

Federal Financial Institutions Examination Council

The largest single concentration of this data is disseminated by the Federal Financial Institutions Examination Council (FFIEC, www.ffiec.gov), an interagency council that brings together all of the federal agencies with an oversight interest in financial institutions: the Federal Deposit Insurance Corporation (FDIC), the National Credit Union Administration (NCUA), the Office of the Comptroller of the Currency (OCC), and the Consumer Financial Protection Bureau (CFPB). The FFIEC Central Data Repository's Public Data Distribution site (https://cdr.ffiec.gov/public/) makes available data on individual commercial and savings banks (but not credit unions or investment banks), including data on various types of income, expenses, assets, and liabilities; amounts of deposits held in various categories; amounts of loans made in various categories; and amounts of loans that have been charged off. The data is available in two ways: users can search for and download human-readable information on individual banks, or they can download large data sets with all of the information for every bank for a given time period.[1]

The FFIEC also distributes data generated from the reports submitted by lenders to comply with the Home Mortgage Disclosure Act (www.ffiec.gov/hmda/hmdaproducts.htm). Data is available at the level of individual loans from 2009 to present, with a lag of about two years; aggregate data at the lender, metropolitan statistical area (MSA), and national level are available from 1999 to present, again with a lag of about two years. For each loan or loan application, the data reports amount of the loan; race, ethnicity, gender, and income of the borrower; location of the property (metropolitan statistical area, state, county, and Census tract); if the loan was denied, the reason for the denial; and additional information about the type of loan and type of property. The aggregate data is also available broken down by many of these parameters.

National Credit Union Administration

The FFIEC does not distribute data about credit unions; that data is handled by the NCUA, the agency that oversees credit unions (www.ncua.gov/DataApps/Pages/default.aspx). The data disseminated by the NCUA for credit unions is similar to the data disseminated by the FFIEC for banks: information about amounts of loans, investments, and other assets held by the credit unions; credit unions' income and expenses in various categories; amounts of delinquent and charged-off loans; and so on. Additional data is available on other topics, including number of current members and number of potential members. Data is available from 1994 to present. As with the bank data, users can search for data on individual credit unions, or they can download files with data on all credit unions for a given quarter.

Office of the Comptroller of the Currency
(U.S. Department of the Treasury)

The Office of the Comptroller of the Currency (OCC) oversees national banks (those chartered by the federal government, as opposed to the typically smaller banks chartered by state governments). Nevertheless, much of the data on national banks is actually reported on the FFIEC's Central Data Repository Public Data Distribution site. One data series that is disseminated via the OCC site is data from the Survey of Credit Underwriting Practices (access via www.occ.gov/publications/), an annual survey in which the lending practices of large national banks are examined for changes in underwriting standards and credit risks. Data is available online from 1998 to present.

MAJOR SOURCES: WORLD

There is little comprehensive, global information on banks and banking. Some useful and interesting data on the bank industry and aggregate lending is available, although it is primarily for developed and upper-middle-income countries.

Financial Access Survey (International Monetary Fund)

One truly global source for international banking data is the Financial Access Survey, which is carried out by the International Monetary Fund (IMF, http://fas.imf.org). This survey looks specifically at banking from the perspectives of households and small and medium-sized businesses. Questions address physical access to banking services (e.g., number of bank branches in the country's three largest cities, number of ATMs per 1,000 square kilometers), actual penetration of banking services (e.g., number of adults per 1,000 who have bank accounts or bank loans, percentage of GDP deposited in banks or other types of financial institutions), and availability of banking services to small and medium-sized businesses (e.g., percentage of bank accounts and bank loans held by small and medium-sized businesses). Data is available from 2004 to present for almost all countries, but there are significant gaps in the coverage for some variables.

Bank for International Settlements

The Bank for International Settlements (BIS, www.bis.org/statistics/index.htm) and its Committee on Payment and Settlement Systems (CPSS) publish statistics on many topics related to international finance, covering its approximately forty member countries. These members include many developed countries (e.g., United States, Germany, Japan), some developing countries (e.g., India, Mexico, Turkey), and some small territories that nevertheless are important in international banking (e.g., Cayman Islands, Hong Kong). The data covers topics related to international finance itself—for example, international lending by banks—and comparative data about the financial systems of countries who are members of the BIS or CPSS, such as per-capita annual usage of checks and debit cards.

Organisation for Economic Co-operation and Development

Another source primarily covering developed countries is the Organisation for Economic Co-operation and Development (OECD), which publishes aggregate data on the income, expenses, assets, and liabilities of various classes of banks (e.g., all commercial banks, only foreign commercial banks, cooperative banks). Data about the number of banks, branches, and employees is also available, broken down by the same classes of banks. This data is available for more than thirty countries, primarily in Europe but also including Chile, Mexico, Israel, Turkey, Japan, South Korea, New Zealand, and the United States. Up to thirty years of time-series data is available for some countries. Access to this data is via OECD StatExtracts (http://stats.oecd.org; see chapter 2).

MINOR SOURCES

Australian Prudential Regulation Authority
Reserve Bank of New Zealand

Australia and New Zealand are two of the few Anglophone countries besides the United States to disseminate bank-level microdata. The Australian Prudential Regulation Authority (APRA), publishes monthly data about specific classes of assets, including various types of loans, of individual banks operating in Australia, 2002 to present (www.apra.gov.au/Pages/default.aspx, "Authorized Deposit-taking Institutions" tab). Data about liabilities, including deposits from households, financial and nonfinancial corporations, and governments, is also available, covering the same time period. The data disseminated by the Reserve Bank of New Zealand (www.rbnz.govt.nz/statistics/banksys/) uses different metrics to report on banks' financial health, including their profitability by various measures, credit rating, capital adequacy, and impaired assets. This data is available from 1996 to present. Some aggregate data is also available for New Zealand banks, covering the same time period.

NOTE

1. The data downloads as a compressed file without a file extension, but opening it with standard unzipping software result in tab-delimited data files.

15
Economics—Real Estate

REAL ESTATE IS AN UNUSUAL ITEM IN THE ECONOMY. IT IS ONE of the few products that are usually bought used rather than newly manufactured, so manufacturing statistics do not adequately capture it, and the land that is part of many real estate transactions is typically not manufactured at all. Housing is often one of the largest pieces of a household's budget, especially for lower-income households, so questions about housing affordability are important politically and socially as well as economically. And, as was demonstrated during the recent financial crisis, economic problems beginning in the housing industry have an effect on the entire economy. The resources in this chapter can help users examine all economic aspects of residential real estate, including trends in home prices, housing affordability, housing quality, and the mortgage market.

MAJOR SOURCES: UNITED STATES

Census Bureau (U.S. Department of Commerce)

The American Housing Survey, managed by the U.S. Census Bureau, is the major source for data about renters, homeowners, and the structures they occupy in the United States. The data covers all aspects of housing, including detailed information about mortgages (amount, interest rate, term, etc.), reasons people gave for moving into their present neighborhood and their present home, problems with their home (e.g., "sagging roof" or "inadequate insulation") or with their neighborhood (e.g., "noise" or "litter"), and even whether the home's smoke detectors are battery-powered or AC. Aggregate data from the American Housing Survey is available through American FactFinder (see chapter 2), but microdata from the survey can be downloaded from the website of the U.S. Department of Housing and Urban Development (HUD, www.huduser.org/portal/datasets/ahs.html). HUD also distributes other housing-related data sets, including data on housing affordability; fair market rents; persons and Census tracts eligible for certain types of HUD assistance; building permits at the state, county, and, in some urban areas, even the town or township level; and number of vacant addresses at the Census tract level.

MAJOR SOURCES: WORLD

Bank for International Settlements

The Bank for International Settlements (BIS, see chapter 14) disseminates data about real estate prices for more than forty countries, plus Hong Kong and the Euro area (www.bis.org/statistics/pp.htm). The data covers most European and North American countries, several countries in east and southeast Asia, plus Australia, New Zealand, Israel, Turkey, and South Africa. Not all of the data sets are strictly comparable: much of the data is indexed (expressed as changes in the price relative to the price on a given date, rather than as actual prices), but the base year varies; some data is seasonally adjusted and some is not; some covers entire countries, some covers only capital cities or urban areas; and the exact type of real estate covered varies from apartments to single-family houses to land. Check the metadata carefully to understand exactly what is covered by the data for any given country.

Eurostat (European Union)

For the European Union, a similar index is available from Eurostat as part of its harmonized indices of consumer prices series (http://epp.eurostat.ec.europa.eu/; search for "HICP—housing" in the Statistical Database). Monthly and annual data on changes in rental prices is also available as part of HICP; search for "harmonised index of consumer prices" in the Statistical Database, click on the "data explorer" icon next to the desired data set (monthly or annual data, index or rate of change), then click on the plus icon next to "All items HICP" and search for "actual rentals for housing." Unlike the BIS data, this data is harmonized and safely comparable across countries, though the BIS may have a longer time series for some European countries. Eurostat makes recent data available only for the housing price index, and data only from 1996 to present for changes in rents. BIS data, on the other hand, is available as far back as 1819 (no, that's not a typo!) for Norway and 1955 for Japan.

MINOR SOURCES

Freddie Mac
Federal Housing Finance Agency

Several U.S. data sources are primarily concerned with the cost of purchasing a home. These include Freddie Mac (also known as the Federal Home Loan Mortgage Corporation), a "government-sponsored enterprise" (GSE) that buys mortgage loans from banks and other lenders. Freddie Mac manages the Primary Mortgage Market Survey (www.freddiemac.com/pmms/), a weekly survey that has been gathering information about mortgage rates since 1971. The entire data set—more than forty years of time-series data—is available on Freddie Mac's website, as is the entire data set converted into a monthly rather than weekly format. Freddie Mac's regulator, the Federal Housing Finance Agency (FHFA), maintains House Price Indices for the United States as a whole, for individual states, and for individual metropolitan statistical areas (www.fhfa.gov, "House Price Index" tab). Some of this data is contained in FRED (see chapter 8), but some of the more detailed data, such as house price indices for individual mid-sized metropolitan areas, is available only on the FHFA site.

S&P/Case-Shiller Home Price Indices

Standard & Poors maintains a set of home price indices, the S&P/Case-Shiller Home Price Indices (http://us.spindices.com/index-family/real-estate/sp-case-shiller). This index was originally developed by economists Karl Case and Robert Shiller. Although a composite index for the entire United States is available, the S&P/Case-Shiller indices primarily focus on conditions in twenty large cities, including New York, Miami, Chicago, Denver, and Los Angeles. Data for some cities is available as far back as 1987. As with the FHFA House Price Index, some of the data sets are in FRED, others, such as the condominium price index, are available only on the S&P site.

National Association of Realtors

Another source of data on home sales in the United States is the National Association of Realtors (NAR, www.realtor.org/research-and-statistics), a trade association for people who work in the real estate industry. In both PDF reports and downloadable Excel spreadsheets, the NAR provides data on sales of existing (not newly constructed) homes, affordability of buying a home, and state of the commercial real estate market, as well as statistics on many other topics related to buying and selling houses. Much of the data is freely available, but some research reports are available only for a fee.

Land Registry
Lloyd's Banking Group

In the United Kingdom, two sources—one private and one governmental—provide geographically detailed data on house prices and house sales. The government source, the Land Registry, publishes data on number of sales per month, average sale price, monthly and annual rate of change in the price, and an overall House Price Index. This data is available as precise as the borough level for the greater London area and at the county level for the rest of England and Wales, 1995 to present. The data is available both as easily searchable, graphically presented statistics (www.landregistry.gov.uk/public/house-prices-and-sales) and as raw data that can be downloaded for further analysis (www.landregistry.gov.uk/market-trend-data/public-data).

Lloyds Banking Group (www.lloydsbankinggroup.com), a private company, publishes its own index, the Halifax House Price Index. This index covers a longer time period than the Land Registry—1983 to present—but offers less geographic detail, with data broken down only by the major geographic regions of the United Kingdom. The Halifax House Price Index does, however, include some data not available from the Land Registry: it has data for Scotland and Northern Ireland and also offers data that separates first-time home buyers from those who are not.

Quotable Value Ltd.

Some detailed home price data is available for New Zealand from Quotable Value Ltd. (QV, www.qv.co.nz/property-info/property-reports/). It provides both a monthly Residential Price Index and a Quarterly House Price Index at the local council level, as well as quarterly data by local council about the number of houses, apartments, and empty lots ("sections") sold and the average price, both overall and for each type of property. Semiannual data is also available for commercial properties and for various types of farmland. Only current data—not time-series data—is provided for some variables.

16
Economics—Trade and Tariffs

As anyone who has paid attention to a presidential campaign in the United States knows, trade is both an economic and a political issue. The sources in this chapter contain data both on the volume of international trade—the values and quantities of goods and, to a lesser extent, services that are created in one country and then sent to another—and on tariffs, trade agreements, and other politically enacted policies that attempt to restrict or encourage international trade.

MAJOR SOURCES: UNITED STATES

Responsibility for international trade statistics in the United States is divided between three divisions of the U.S. Department of Commerce: the Census Bureau and the International Trade Administration both disseminate statistics on international trade in tangible goods, and the Bureau of Economic Analysis disseminates data on trade in services and intangible goods. Collectively, they distribute trade data through several different sites.

Census Bureau
(U.S. Department of Commerce)

The Census Bureau's Foreign Trade website (www.census.gov/foreign-trade/index.html) bills itself as "the official source for U.S. export and import statistics." Its data on the value of imports and exports is available in the following ways:

- Overall annual data on trade between the United States and the rest of the world is available 1960 to present (www.census.gov/foreign-trade/statistics/historical/).
- Monthly and annual data on overall trade (total imports, total exports, and trade balance) between the United States and individual foreign countries, territories, or regions of the world is available 1985 to present for many countries, with shorter time series available for territories (www.census.gov/foreign-trade/statistics/country/).
- In the "U.S. International Trade Statistics" section, one can find detailed monthly data about trade between the United States and individual foreign countries in specific products, 2000 to present (http://censtats.census.gov/naic3_6/naics3_6.shtml).
- Additional monthly data on trade in "advanced technology products," such as computer and electronic equipment, certain medical products, and aerospace products, is available 1989 to present for overall import and export data, and 2003 to present for data broken down by country and type of product (www.census.gov/foreign-trade/statistics/country/).

Additionally, statistics about U.S.-based companies that are involved in importing and exporting are available 1987 to present, with gaps (www.census.gov/foreign-trade/aip/index.html#profile).

Another Census Bureau site, known as the NAICS Related-Party database (http://sasweb.ssd.census.gov/relatedparty/), may be useful for researchers who want annual rather than monthly time series of trade data in specific products. Like the "U.S. International Trade Statistics" site mentioned previously, it provides data about trade between the United States and any given foreign country in specific products—down to six-digit NAICS codes (see chapter 1 for an explanation of NAICS codes). It has only annual data, and only for 2002 to present, but unlike the "U.S. International Trade Statistics" site it allows users to download data for multiple time periods at once. It also allows users to separate out trade involving related parties (where the importer has a substantial equity stake in the exporter or vice versa).

International Trade Administration
(U.S. Department of Commerce)

TradeStats Express (TSE, http://tse.export.gov), which is produced by the International Trade Administration (ITA), contains quarterly and annual data on trade between the United States and foreign countries, 1989 to present. This data is available either at the level of the entire United States or of individual states, and, on the other side of the trade, at the level of individual countries, of continents or other large regions, or of countries belonging to various international groups such as the European Union, Organization of Petroleum Exporting Countries (OPEC), and Association of Southeast Asian Nations (ASEAN). Although the NAICS Related-Party database and the TSE both disseminate data based on the same administrative sources (viz., electronic declarations filed by exporters and importers with the U.S. Census Bureau and U.S. Customs and Border Protection), the two report slightly different figures. The NAICS Related-Party database includes only imports for consumption (i.e., imports on which customs duties have been paid and which are available to be used or sold in the United States), whereas the TSE also includes imports that are being held in "bonded warehouses" or "Foreign Trade Zones." These are special areas where imported goods can be stored without incurring customs duties until they become "imports for consumption" or are reexported elsewhere without customs duties. Additionally, the databases handle seasonal adjustments, errata, and certain other technical matters differently. Refer to the documentation for both databases for specific information about how each one arrives at the numbers it reports.

Bureau of Economic Analysis
(U.S. Department of Commerce)

The Bureau of Economic Analysis (BEA) publishes data on trade in services (e.g., education, insurance, consulting) and intangible goods (e.g., royalties and similar payments on intellectual property) between the United States and approximately thirty major trading partners. Much of the data, which is available on its "International Economic Accounts" site (www.bea.gov/international/index.htm), covers 1986 to present, although some data sets cover shorter periods of time. Beginning with 2006, data is also available broken down into trade between unaffiliated entities, trade between U.S. affiliates and foreign parent companies, and trade between foreign affiliates and U.S. parent companies.

U.S. International Trade Commission

Another source for U.S. trade data, as well as data on the amount of tariffs and other duties paid on that trade, is the International Tariff and Trade DataWeb (http://dataweb.usitc.gov; free registration required), produced by the U.S. International Trade Commission. This source provides more detailed measures of the value of imports than many other sources; it has several different measures of value that variously include or exclude costs such as insurance on the merchandise, freight for shipping the merchandise, and amount of import duties paid on the merchandise. The estimated ("calculated") amount of duties paid is also available as a separate variable, as is the actual quantity of goods imported or exported. The site offers many options for defining groups of products, including NAICS, the Standard Industrial Classification (SIC), the Standard International Trade Classification (SITC), and the Harmonized Tariff Schedule (HTS, a U.S.-based expansion of the Harmonized System; see chapter 1 for more information about the various codes used to classify trade data). Data is available at the most specific level offered by each of the classification systems, which allows users to select fine-grained product categories. Data is available monthly, 1989 to present.

USA Trade Online (U.S. Census Bureau)

Foreign trade data is one of the few types of data produced by the federal government that is not always free to users; some of the Census Bureau's foreign trade data products require a subscription. These include those available via USA Trade Online (https://usatrade.census.gov), which has monthly import and export data with finer geographic detail than other Census Bureau products; users can download data at the level of individual ports as well as districts (groups of ports in the same general geographic area). Another advantage of USA Trade Online is that, like the International Tariff and Trade DataWeb and unlike many other U.S. federal trade data sources, it provides data on the quantity as well as the value of imports and exports. Although USA Trade Online generally requires a subscription, it can be freely accessed by anyone at some federal depository libraries.

MAJOR SOURCES: WORLD

United Nations Conference on Trade and Development

The United Nations Conference on Trade and Development (UNCTAD) disseminates data through several different sources, including three useful databases: UNCTADstat, Comtrade, and TRAINS.

UNCTADstat (http://unctadstat.unctad.org). The UNCTADstat website provides a great deal of data on trade, foreign direct investment, exchange rates, shipping, and other topics related to countries' economic relationships with the rest of the world. Some data is available as far back as 1948, including the overall value of imports and exports for most countries. To view data in UNCTADstat, first find the report containing the needed data, either by searching or by browsing through the tree structure. After you click on the report's title, a table opens with default settings, often showing global or regional data. To view data for individual countries, click on "ECONOMY," which displays options for selecting either individual countries or various groupings of countries, such as "least developed countries," "landlocked developing countries," or "ECOWAS" (Economic Community of West African States). Click on "Show table" to return to the data view. Similarly, clicking on any of the other underlined headings, such as "PARTNER" (for trade partners), "YEAR," or "PRODUCT," displays options for choosing different parameters for those variables. Products are classified by SITC codes.

Comtrade (the name stands for "Commodity Trade Statistics Database"; http://comtrade.un.org). Comtrade provides extremely detailed data on the value and quantity of exports, imports, reexports, and reimports between approximately two hundred countries, territories, and economic groupings, 1962 to present. Data is available classified by both SITC and Harmonized System (HS) codes as well as Broad Economic Categories (BEC). The data sets classified by HS codes are available down to the six-digit level, which makes them some of the most detailed trade data available internationally. For example, the HS-classified data in Comtrade includes not merely trade in cheese—the most detailed cheese-related category in NAICS—but specifically blue-veined cheese, fresh cheese, grated/powdered cheese, and processed cheese. Because the data is so fine-grained and is available for so many years, more than a billion data points are available in the database. However, only 50,000 of them can be downloaded at a time, so users may have to query strategically to assemble large data sets.

UNCTAD TRAINS (Trade Analysis and Information System). This source is focused on data about tariffs and other trade control measures. Access to TRAINS is provided by the World Integrated Trade Solution (WITS, http://wits.worldbank.org/wits/), an online system that can also be used to access Comtrade and some additional trade-related data. The TRAINS data is very granular; tariff data is available at the ten-digit HS level when using the "Quick Search" options, or at the six-digit HS level when using the "Advanced Query" interface, covering both bound duties (the legal maximum duty on a given item) and applied duties (the duty actually in effect at a given point in time). In addition to the standard data queries and download capabilities, WITS provides sophisticated options for working with the data online, including the ability to save queries between sessions, create custom groupings of products and countries that can be saved and used in queries, and model changes in the amount of trade based on hypothetical changes in the tariffs applied to that trade. Bulk data downloads are also available for the TRAINS data, 1988 to present. Although the WITS system has many useful capabilities, it does have a few drawbacks. A free registration is required, and the system can be slow to process some queries and make the data files available for download.

MINOR SOURCES

World Trade Organization

Trade data is available from several international and regional organizations. The World Trade Organization (WTO), despite its name, is not an especially good source of trade data; its activities primarily focus on trade negotiations and disputes. It does, however, have good data on trade agreements, including a regional trade agreement (RTA) database (http://rtais.wto.org/UI/PublicMaintainRTAHome.aspx) and a preferential trade agreement (PTA) database (http://ptadb.wto.org/?lang=1). It also provides some recent data on trade, as well as data on tariff rates (www.wto.org/english/res_e/statis_e/data_pub_e.htm). The data on tariffs, disseminated via the WTO's Tariff Analysis Online site (TAO, http://tariffanalysis.wto.org/?ui=1; free registration required), is copious and multifaceted, covering both bound and applied duties as well as quotas affecting tariffs, subsidies provided by countries to exporters of various products, and more. Be aware, though, that not all countries' data is included in TAO. Also, the TAO time series are not as lengthy as those available from some other sources: TAO contains only data 1996 to present; WITS has data 1988 to present, for example.

World Bank

In addition to the basic trade data it publishes on the World Bank Data site (http://data.worldbank.org; see chapter 2), the World Bank publishes the Exporter Dynamics Database (http://data.worldbank.org/data-catalog/exporter-dynamics-database; click "DATABANK" in the right sidebar to access aggregate data). This database contains information about companies that export products from a given country, such as average value of products exported per company, average number of different types of products exported per company, and average number of countries to which a company exports. Much of this data is available broken down by companies that are new entrants to the market, those exiting the market, and incumbents. Data is available for forty-five countries, 1997–2011.

Regional Organizations

Several regional or other groups provide trade databases that primarily contain data specifically from their member states. These include DataIntal, from the InterAmerican Development Bank (www.iadb.org/dataintal/); Comext, from the European Union (http://epp.eurostat.ec.europa.eu/newxtweb/); and multiple data sets from the Organisation for Economic Co-operation and Development (OECD, http://stats.oecd.org). For the most part, the data points contained in these data sets are simply subsets of the data available from the global sources mentioned previously, with some variations in definitions, time periods available, and the like.

One OECD data set deserves individual mention. The Trade in Value Added (TiVA) data set is a recently initiated joint project of the WTO and OECD. Unlike most trade statistics, the TiVA data (http://stats.oecd.org/; search for TiVA) takes into account the fact that many exported items are not entirely manufactured in a single country. For example, a pair of jeans exported from Bangladesh might be made from cotton imported from India and zippers imported from Japan. This causes problems for traditional trade statistics; to name just one, the value of the cotton and the zippers gets double-counted in global trade figures, once when they are exported from India and Japan, respectively, and again when they are exported from Bangladesh as part of the finished jeans. Traditional trade statistics also make it difficult to estimate just how much Bangladesh's economy benefits from exporting that pair of jeans. To solve problems such as this, the data in TiVA would include only the value added in Bangladesh.[1]

NOTE

1. For example, if the cotton cost $5, the zippers cost $1, and the jeans were worth $20, TiVA would attribute $14 in exports to Bangladesh ($20 total value minus $5 worth of components imported from India minus $1 worth of components imported from Japan = $14 in value added in Bangladesh). The data in TiVA is not yet comprehensive; as of the May 2013 release only fifty-six countries and the European Union were included, and only selected years between 1995 and 2009 were covered.

17
Education

THIS CHAPTER REVIEWS SOURCES ON PRESCHOOL, K–12, AND higher education, including data about the schools and teachers providing that education and the performance and demographics of the students participating in it. Data about educational attainment—how much formal schooling an adult has completed—is not covered in this chapter. Educational attainment is a common question on American demographic and workforce surveys, including the Decennial Census, the Current Population Survey, and the American Community Survey; see chapters 2 and 20 for more information on accessing these data sets. Globally, educational attainment data is available from the UNdata site (http://data.un.org) and from many regional data sources, also covered in chapter 2.

MAJOR SOURCES: UNITED STATES

National Center for Education Statistics
(U.S. Department of Education)

The National Center for Education Statistics (NCES, http://nces.ed.gov) is the major federal source for data about education at all levels in the United States, from pre-kindergarten through graduate school. It also collects extensive data about libraries in the United States.

Some of the most commonly requested data about K–12 education is in the NCES Common Core of Data (CCD, http://nces.ed.gov/ccd/), which contains information about every public school district and public school in the country. Available data sets include number of students, teachers, librarians, guidance counselors, aides, administrators, and other categories of staff; demographic information about enrolled students in each grade, students receiving a high school diploma, students completing high school without receiving a diploma, and the general population of the district; dropout rates and graduation rates; number of students who receive free or reduced-price school lunches, have an individualized education program (IEP), or are migrant students or English-language learners; total and per-student expenditures in various categories; detailed data about the district's sources of revenue; and district's long-term and short-term debt. Some of the data is available as far back as 1986. The Common Core of Data does not, however, include data about student or school performance, such as standardized test scores or the fraction of students considered proficient in various subjects.

NCES maintains a similarly comprehensive data set for colleges and universities, the Integrated Postsecondary Education Data System (IPEDS, http://nces.ed.gov/ipeds/). As with the CCD, this data set contains information about number of students and faculty, demographics of enrolled students, retention and graduation rates, and detailed information about sources of revenues and types of expenditures. Other data tracks cost of attendance; demographic, tenure, salary, and fringe benefits information for instructional staff; demographic and salary information for other staff; information about the college or university's endowment, other assets, and liabilities; amount of financial aid awarded in various categories; fraction of students receiving aid; student loan default rates; percentage of students with disabilities; number of students in various fields; admissions rates; test scores; and number of students who play varsity sports. Some data is available as far back as 1980.

NCES runs one study of student performance, the National Assessment of Educational Progress (NAEP, http://nces.ed.gov/nationsreportcard/). This study provides data about students' average scores on tests of various subjects including reading, mathematics, U.S. and world history, and foreign language. Data is available broken down by various demographic factors such as gender, race, disability status, parents' education, English proficiency, and eligibility for free or reduced-price school lunches. Data can also be broken down by state, and, for a few large districts, by school district.

Additionally, NCES has run several longitudinal studies in which they follow a small cohort of students or teachers for many years. These include the Early Childhood Longitudinal Study (which has, at different times, followed children from birth through kindergarten, kindergarten through eighth grade, and kindergarten through fifth grade), the Beginning Teacher Longitudinal Study, and other studies that have followed students from high school into adulthood. NCES also runs national surveys on specialized topics such as crime in schools, career and technical education, and private schools. Much of the data from these studies is available on the NCES site, although the availability of some segments of the microdata is restricted.

MAJOR SOURCES: WORLD

United Nations Educational, Social and Cultural Organization

Internationally, the United Nations Educational, Social and Cultural Organization's (UNESCO) Institute for Statistics (www.uis.unesco.org) is the most comprehensive collection of education statistics, including preschool and tertiary (college level) education. The data, which is available primarily at the country level (in some cases, regional level), covers number of students enrolled and teachers employed in different levels of education; percentage of teachers at different levels of education who are female; ratio of students enrolled in school to all school-aged children at different levels of education; number of school-aged children who are not in school; graduation rates; rates at which students repeat grades; percentage of children receiving technical or vocational education at various levels; percentage of children who attend private schools at various levels; percentage of children from a country who are attending school in another country; percentage of children attending school in a country who are not from that country; number and percentage of students majoring in various subjects in tertiary education; spending on education at various levels; and more. UNESCO also provides detailed demographic breakdowns for common indicators such as literacy rates and the fraction of children enrolled in school. (Both are indicators for the Millennium Development Goals and thus widely reported in general statistics sources.) For some countries and some variables, data is available as far back as 1970.

Programme for International Student Assessment
(Organisation for Economic Co-operation and Development)

Trends in International Mathematics and Science Study
(Boston College)

Progress in International Reading Literacy Study
(Boston College)

Internationally comparable student performance data—what students in different countries, on average, have learned—is available from a handful of sources: the OECD Programme for International Student Assessment (PISA, www.oecd.org/pisa/) and Trends in International Mathematics and

Science Study (TIMSS) and Progress in International Reading Literacy Study (PIRLS, both at http://timssandpirls.bc.edu). PISA tests students 15 and 16 years old on three subjects: reading, mathematics, and science. PIRLS is given to students in the fourth grade and tests only reading. TIMSS is given to students in the fourth and eighth grades and tests both mathematics and science. All three have short time series available: PISA data is available every three years from 2000–2012. TIMSS data is available every fourth year from 1995 onward, and PIRLS data is available every fifth year from 2001 onward. For all three tests, patrons can access reports and tables containing statistics, as well as the microdata (individual students' answers to individual questions). Unfortunately, not all countries participate in any or all of these tests; when one of these tests is administered, fifty to seventy countries or parts of countries typically participate. European, Middle Eastern, and Asian countries tend to be well represented, but few sub-Saharan African countries take part.

Although the main purpose of these tests is to assess students' academic skills, PISA, TIMSS, and PIRLS also include questions that go beyond academic performance. All three ask questions about the students' home life and family background, such as their parents' jobs and education levels; number of books and availability of a computer and an Internet connection in the home; and availability of dedicated workspace for the student at home. TIMSS and PIRLS also ask whether students have experienced any of six specific aspects of bullying behavior at school: being teased, being excluded by fellow students, being slandered, being forced to do things against their will by fellow students, being assaulted by fellow students, and having items stolen. All three studies also ask if students enjoy or think they are good at activities such as reading or studying math and science and investigate students' attitudes toward their schools and their teachers. PISA includes questions on students' studying strategies and on how much time they spend on tutoring or other academic lessons outside of school.

All three studies also ask adults involved in a child's education to complete a survey as well: TIMSS and PIRLS survey teachers and principals; PISA surveys parents and principals. The principal surveys in all three studies ask both objective questions, such as the school's enrollment, and more subjective questions, such as whether they feel that their school has shortages of various types of resources or how serious of a problem they consider various disciplinary issues to be at their school. The teacher survey in TIMSS and PIRLS includes similar questions about shortages and problems as well as questions about the teacher's professional background and teaching methods. PISA's parent survey asks about educational activities the parents participate in with their child as well as their own reading habits and attitudes toward reading and toward their child's school. The microdata from the teacher, principal, and parent surveys is also available. Identifiers allow the teacher, principal, parent, and student surveys to be linked, so researchers can, for example, see if principals' and teachers' assessments of shortages in the same schools are the same, or whether parents' reading habits correlate with their children's test scores.

MINOR SOURCES

State Departments of Education

Education has historically been overseen at the state level rather than the federal level in the United States, and even today the richest educational data is often distributed by state-level departments of education, not by the U.S. Department of Education. This is especially true for data about student or school performance, such as standardized test scores, percentage of students meeting proficiency standards, and which schools are showing "adequate yearly progress"; these standards are defined, monitored, and reported primarily at the state level, not nationally. The easiest way to find this data for individual schools or school districts is to search each state's department of education website.

Other International Projects

TIMSS, PIRLS, and PISA are not the only efforts to create internationally comparable data on student performance and school effectiveness. The Southern and Eastern Africa Consortium for Monitoring Educational Quality (SACMEQ, www.sacmeq.org), which has data from the late 1990s to the present for several African countries, is a smaller regional effort toward the same ends. A group of European economists lead by Nadir Altinok used data from all of these assessments and others to create standardized estimates of educational performance for more than one hundred countries, 1965–2010, although estimates are not available for all countries for all years (www.beta-umr7522.fr/Datasets/).

Department for Education (U.K.)

The U.K. government has extensive, easily accessible data on primary and secondary education in England, distributed through its Department for Education (www.gov.uk/dfe, but site is in the process of moving). A smaller amount of data about education in Wales and Scotland is published on the websites of the Welsh (http://wales.gov.uk) and Scottish (www.scotland.gov.uk) governments, respectively. The data about individual schools and districts is similar to that available in the NCES Common Core of Data for the United States: number of students by age and ethnicity; number of students who receive free school lunches; number of students whose first language is not English; number of students with special needs; number of teachers, teaching assistants, librarians, and other types of staff; and expenses, revenues, and per-student spending. Additionally, there is data on student performance, specifically the percentage of students who perform at various levels on tests at key stages, including the General Certificate of Secondary Education (GCSE) level.

18
Energy

THE SOURCES IN THIS CHAPTER PROVIDE DATA ON THE CONSUMPTION, production of, and trade in energy, including petroleum products, coal, electricity, and alternative fuels. This chapter also contains some data about the emission of greenhouse gases by the energy industry, but broader data about greenhouse gas emissions can be obtained from the sources discussed in chapter 6.

MAJOR SOURCES: UNITED STATES

Energy Information Administration (U.S. Department of Energy)

The U.S. Energy Information Administration (EIA, www.eia.gov) is an excellent source of information, not only for domestic data about energy production, usage, and prices but also for international data. Some data goes as far back as 1899 (proved reserves of crude oil) or 1949 (e.g., domestic energy production and consumption data; prices, exports, and imports for various types of fuels; heating and cooling degree-days); other data goes as far into the future as 2035 (projections of the demand for and production of various types of energy, both internationally and domestically). Carbon dioxide emission information is also available back to 1973. Much of the data on the EIA site is organized by type of fuel, with links to EIA publications with statistics about that product, but data is also available organized by geographic area.

MAJOR SOURCES: WORLD

United Nations Statistics Division

There is no UN agency that corresponds to the U.S. Energy Information Administration, but the United Nations Statistics Division does gather data on energy production and consumption as well as trade in energy-related products. This data, which covers 1990 to the present, is available through the UNdata site (http://data.un.org; see chapter 2). The data sets include figures for the production, consumption, and trade of different fuels, including several petroleum products (e.g., crude oil, liquefied petroleum gas, petroleum coke), several varieties of coal (e.g., hard coal, lignite, brown coal coke), as well as electricity generated by wind, solar, hydro, ocean tides or waves, and nuclear power. Data on refined fuels such as regular gasoline, aviation gasoline, kerosene, diesel, and biodiesel is also available, as is data on energy produced from several different kinds of wastes (e.g., municipal waste, pulp and paper waste).

MINOR SOURCES

Organization of Petroleum Exporting Countries
International Energy Agency

There are two major international organizations with an interest in energy-related data: the Organization of Petroleum Exporting Countries (OPEC, www.opec.org) and the International Energy Agency (IEA, www.iea.org). Neither has a particularly large membership.

OPEC has twelve members (Algeria, Angola, Ecuador, Iran, Iraq, Kuwait, Libya, Nigeria, Qatar, Saudi Arabia, the United Arab Emirates, and Venezuela), which collectively account for more than 40 percent of annual crude oil production in the world. OPEC statistics are focused primarily on member states' activities, but they include some data on other countries, particularly major oil- and gas-exporting countries such as Russia, Canada, the United States, and the United Kingdom. The OPEC annual report contains some data that is hard to find from other free sources, such as the average spot prices of various specific types of crude oil (e.g., Iran heavy or West Texas intermediate).

The IEA has twenty-eight members (most of the countries in western and central Europe, plus Turkey, the United States, Canada, Australia, New Zealand, Japan, and South Korea). It disseminates some basic data for all countries in the world, including recent data on the production and consumption of energy from various sources, on energy imports and exports, and on carbon dioxide emissions from burning certain types of fuels. Although detailed data (including time series) is available only for a fee via the IEA site, some IEA time-series data is freely distributed through the World Bank Data portal (see chapter 2).

U.S. Environmental Protection Agency

The U.S. Environmental Protection Agency (EPA) disseminates detailed data on the emission of air pollutants and greenhouse gases by the electric power industry for 1990 to the present, with a lag of several years. Via the Emissions and Generation Resource Integrated Database (eGRID, www.epa.gov/cleanenergy/energy-resources/egrid/index.html), users can find plant-level and even boiler-level data on the type of fuel used and amount of pollution emitted. This includes both full-year annual data and "ozone season"–only data on the total emissions of several important pollutants, such as sulfur dioxide, carbon dioxide, and nitrogen oxides, as well as data on the amount emitted per input (in British thermal units) and output (in megawatt-hours).

19

Health and Health Care

THE SOURCES IN THIS CHAPTER CONTAIN DATA ON ALL ASPECTS of health and health care, including nutrition, mental health, dental care, and financial aspects of the health care system, along with data on physical illnesses from cancer to cholera. For the purposes of this book, substance abuse is also considered to be a health issue, and data sources on that topic are included in this chapter as well. Some sources for data about births and deaths are included in this chapter, but additional sources for those topics can be found in chapter 20 with other sources for demographic data.

MAJOR SOURCES: UNITED STATES

National Center for Health Statistics

The National Center for Health Statistics (NCHS, www.cdc.gov/nchs/), a department within the Centers for Disease Control (CDC), distributes an almost overwhelming amount of data on the health status of Americans, gathered and disseminated through many programs. The data ranges in complexity from simple statistics—say, the number of people diagnosed with whooping cough per year—published in FastStats (www.cdc.gov/nchs/fastats/), to massive raw data sets produced by the following three major ongoing survey projects:

National Health and Nutrition Examination Survey (NHANES, www.cdc.gov/nchs/nhanes.htm). For this survey, individuals are asked about many aspects of their health and wellness: the foods they eat, how much sleep they get, how frequently they exercise, the last time they saw a dentist, what kind of health insurance they have, which prescription medications they take. Individuals are also given a thorough physical examination and a panel of medical tests, including hearing tests, tests of muscle strength, and tests to screen for various diseases. NHANES, which has been conducted in various forms since the 1970s, is the most extensive of the surveys managed by NCHS.

National Health Interview Survey (NHIS, www.cdc.gov/nchs/nhis.htm). This survey asks some questions similar to those in NHANES, concerning health conditions affecting individuals, the kind of health insurance they have, their exercise habits, their access to medical and dental care, and the like. NHIS does not, however, include the same detailed information about food intake, nor does it include any kind of physical examination or medical test. It has been conducted since 1957, although data only from 1963 to present is available to researchers.

National Health Care Surveys (NHCS, www.cdc.gov/nchs/dhcs.htm). Unlike NHANES and NHIS, which gather information from consumers of health care, the surveys within NHCS gather information from providers: hospitals, primary care physicians, nursing homes, home health aides, and others. These surveys contain data about topics such as the number of doctor's visits annually, broken down by various types of physicians and by various demographic groupings, and the reasons for doctor's visits, which are covered by the National Ambulatory Medical Care Survey (NAMCS); the number of emergency room visits, along with characteristics of the patients (e.g., age, gender, race) and of the visit (e.g., wait times, triage status, reason for the visit), which are included in the National Hospital Ambulatory Medical Care Survey (NHAMCS); and the reasons for hospital stays and demographic information about the patients, which are the topics on the National Hospital Care Survey (NHCS; formerly the National Hospital Discharge Survey). In addition to these three ongoing surveys, the NHCS has done intermittent or one-time surveys such as the National Nursing Home Survey, the National Home and Hospice Care Survey, the National Survey of Residential Care Facilities, the National Home Health Aide Survey, and the National Nursing Assistant Survey.

NCHS also manages the National Vital Statistics System (see chapter 20) as well as several smaller surveys. These smaller surveys include the National Survey of Family Growth, which covers topics related to contraception, pregnancy, and sexuality; the National Survey of Children's Health, which surveys parents about their children's health insurance, health care, social and emotional development, activities, and other topics related to their children's physical and mental health; the National Survey of Children with Special Health Care Needs, which covers similar topics but includes only children with physical or mental illnesses, disabilities (including learning disabilities), or developmental delays; and the National Immunization Survey, which gathers information about children's immunization history along with some demographic data. A full list of the types of data collected by various NCHS programs can be found on the NCHS website (www.cdc.gov/nchs/data/factsheets/factsheet_summary.htm).

MAJOR SOURCES: WORLD

World Health Organization

The World Health Organization (for data, www.who.int/research/en/) is the major international source for data on health and health care. Much of its data is distributed through the Global Health Observatory Data Repository (http://apps.who.int/gho/data/), which contains tables of data, typically at the country level, for dozens of indicators, including the incidence of diseases such as cholera, malaria, meningitis, HIV/AIDS, and other sexually transmitted infections; indicators of the quality of the health care system, such as per-capita spending on health care and number of hospitals per 100,000 people; indicators of alcohol and tobacco usage and control, such as whether the government bans smoking in certain types of environments or limits the sale of alcohol to people over a certain age; and environmental factors that impact health, such as UV radiation exposure and air pollution levels.

MINOR SOURCES

Demographic and Health Surveys

Demographic and Health Surveys (DHS, www.dhsprogram.com) is funded by the United States Agency for International Development (USAID) to conduct surveys about maternal and child health, including topics related to family planning, in developing countries. These surveys are a rarity in the world of data, including subnational data for developing countries (data for provinces within countries, not just for the whole country), time series (some countries have six waves of data going back to the late 1980s), and a survey approach that allows measurement of opinions, beliefs, and other factors that are not easily captured by administrative records. Raw data from the surveys is available to users who register with DHS.

Agency for Healthcare Research and Quality
(U.S. Department of Health and Human Services)

In the United States, the Agency for Healthcare Research and Quality (AHRQ), part of the U.S. Department of Health and Human Services, is a good source for economic data about health care (as opposed to data about medical conditions, the major focus of NCHS). It is responsible for two major data collection and dissemination projects, the Medical Expenditure Panel Survey (MEPS, http://meps.ahrq.gov/mepsweb/) and the Healthcare Cost and Utilization Project (HCUP, http://hcupnet.ahrq.gov). MEPS gathers data on the amount of money consumers and businesses spend on various types of health care and health insurance; HCUP collects information about the nature and costs of hospital visits, including emergency room visits. Data is also gathered on outpatient surgeries, but that data is not freely available.

Centers for Disease Control
(U.S. Department of Health and Human Services)

The CDC has several additional data resources beyond those managed by NCHS. The Behavioral Risk Factor Surveillance System (BRFSS, www.cdc.gov/brfss/) is a long-running survey that includes questions about health conditions and behaviors that can impact health, such as eating fruits and vegetables and using seatbelts. Data from BRFSS is available both through user-friendly online databases and as microdata. The Web-based Injury Statistics Query and Reporting System (WISQARS, www.cdc.gov/injury/wisqars/index.html) disseminates detailed data about injuries of all sorts, including fatal and nonfatal injuries both accidental and intentional. The NCHHSTP Atlas (www.cdc.gov/nchhstp/atlas/), produced by the National Center for HIV/AIDS, Viral Hepatitis, STD, and TB Prevention, displays state-level data on the incidence of those diseases. Many other resources can be found by searching the CDC site.

National Cancer Institute (U.S. National Institutes of Health)

One of the best sources for data and statistics about cancer is the Surveillance Epidemiology and End Results Program database (SEER, http://seer.cancer.gov), which is produced by the National Cancer Institute, part of the U.S. National Institutes of Health. Although the raw SEER data is restricted-use, extensive statistics and aggregate data are freely available. The statistics and aggregate data include information about the incidence, prevalence, survival times, and deaths from many types of cancer; this data can be broken down with a great deal of demographic and geographic precision.

Substance Abuse and Mental Health Services Administration
(U.S. Department of Health and Human Services)

Another agency within the Department of Health and Human Services, the Substance Abuse and Mental Health Services Administration (SAMHSA), publishes both aggregate data and microdata about behavioral health issues. The aggregate data, available on its website (www.samhsa.gov/data/), includes quantitative information about drug use among people 12 years and older, gathered via the National Survey on Drug Use and Health (NSDUH); statistics about drug overdoses and other drug-related events that result in deaths or emergency room visits, gathered by the Drug Abuse Warning Network (DAWN); information about facilities that provide treatment for substance abuse and the people who are treated there, gathered by the National Survey of Substance Abuse Treatment Services (N-SSATS) and the Treatment Episode Data Set (TEDS), respectively; and state-level statistics about mental health care. Microdata created by SAMHSA is available in the Substance Abuse and Mental Health Data Archive (SAMHDA, www.icpsr.umich.edu/icpsrweb/SAMHDA/), which is hosted by the Interuniversity Consortium for Political and Social Research.

Interuniversity Consortium for Political and Social Research

The Interuniversity Consortium for Political and Social Research (ICPSR) allows researchers to perform online analyses of data from several NCHS surveys, including NHANES and the National Survey of Family Growth, using Survey Description and Analysis (SDA) software. This feature is freely available, even for researchers who are not affiliated with an ICPSR member institution. Online data analysis is also available for many of the data sets in SAMHDA, NAHDAP, and NACDA, although in some cases access may be limited to ICPSR members. (See appendix B for instructions on using SDA to analyze data online.)

National Institute on Drug Abuse

The National Institute on Drug Abuse, part of the U.S. federal government and housed within the U.S. National Institutes of Health, publishes data on both drug addiction and HIV/AIDS via ICPSR. Its data archive, the National Addiction and HIV Data Archive Program (NAHDAP, www.icpsr.umich.edu/icpsrweb/NAHDAP/index.jsp), contains extensive data on the use of tobacco, alcohol, and other drugs, including drug use among teenagers, prisoners, and other specific populations. One notable survey contained in NAHDAP is "Monitoring the Future: A Continuing Study of the Lifestyles and Values of Youth," which has surveyed high school seniors annually since 1975, and eighth-graders and tenth-graders annually since 1991. The Monitoring the Future Surveys contain questions on alcohol, drugs, smoking, crime, and sex, as well as questions about the place of religion and respondents' parents in their lives, their goals in life, and many other topics.

National Archive of Computerized Data on Aging

Another federally sponsored, health-related data collection hosted at ICPSR is the National Archive of Computerized Data on Aging (NACDA, www.icpsr.umich.edu/icpsrweb/NACDA/), which is sponsored by the National Institute on Aging. It has some data sets on older adults in other countries as well as those in the United States. Some of the data in NACDA is available only to ICPSR subscribers, but much of it is freely available to the general public.

Dartmouth Atlas of Health Care

The Dartmouth Atlas of Health Care (www.dartmouthatlas.org) illustrates geographic disparities in health care utilization in the United States. Most of the data is available on a regional basis; some is also available at the level of counties or of specific hospitals. Available indicators, to name just a few, are average amount of Medicare reimbursements per person enrolled in Medicare, number of knee replacements performed per 1,000 people enrolled in Medicare, and number of hospital beds per 1,000 people in the region. Although the site has a clear rhetorical purpose—to argue that some areas of the country are spending too much on health care, relative to the benefits to the patients—it is still a useful and visually engaging source of data on this topic.

National Health Service (England)

In England, the National Health Service (NHS) publishes remarkably detailed data about the health care it provides through the Health and Social Care Information Centre (www.hscic.gov.uk). This data goes down to the level of individual hospitals or individual practices for some indicators, including number of prescriptions written by general practitioners for various drugs and cost for those prescriptions. Other aggregate data available at the level of individual NHS trusts includes number of emergency room visits, broken down by the patients' genders and ages and by the information about the visit (day of the week, time of arrival, length of visit, etc.); percentage of patients receiving various tests and treatments for various types of cancer; and number of people referred for or receiving psychiatric treatment and some information about the outcome of that treatment. There is also national-level data on drinking and smoking behavior.

Other National Health Agencies

Australia and New Zealand make available substantial health statistics. The Australian Institute of Health and Welfare (AIHW, www.aihw.gov.au) has an extensive array of both statistical publications and data tables and "data cubes," which allow for interactive, online exploration of the data. New Zealand's Ministry of Health (www.health.govt.nz) conducts and reports on a variety of surveys, from the New Zealand Health Survey, which covers many topics related to health and health care, to more focused surveys such as the Nutrition Survey and the Oral Health Survey. Access to microdata from the Ministry of Health Surveys is restricted, but many statistics are available on the ministry's website.

20
People and Households

THIS CHAPTER INCLUDES SOURCES FOR SOCIAL, ECONOMIC, and demographic data on people and households. Some of the most useful databases for topics such as these are general-purpose databases, such as American FactFinder or UNdata (see chapter 2). The databases listed below specifically focus on demography (including vital statistics, which count births and deaths as well as international migration), on the expenditures made by individuals and households, and on the socioeconomic status (education, occupation, income, etc.) of individuals and households. Additional sources for data about the wage and salary income of people can be found in chapter 12.

MAJOR SOURCES: UNITED STATES

Census Bureau (U.S. Department of Commerce)
Bureau of Labor Statistics (U.S. Department of Labor)

American Community Survey (ACS, www.census.gov/acs/www/). This Census Bureau project surveys more than 250,000 residents of the United States each month. These monthly samples are then combined into one-year, three-year, or five-year groupings to estimate the characteristics of the American population during that one-year, three-year, or five-year period. The questions on the survey cover basic demographics (age, gender, race, ethnicity, ancestry, marital status, children, etc.) as well as educational attainment, income, and employment. Less common topics covered by the ACS include transportation (including the number of vehicles possessed by the household and detailed information about commuting methods and times); whether the person moved in the past year and, if so, where they moved from (within the same county, within the same state, or from a different state); whether the person has any disability; what languages are spoken in the household; and each person's citizenship and immigration history. ACS also includes questions about the house itself, including the year it was built, the number of rooms, what fuel is used to heat it, and measures of its affordability. The five-year estimates from the ACS are available for very small geographic areas—as small as individual Census tracts—but the one-year and three-year estimates are available only for larger areas, those with populations over 65,000 and 20,000, respectively. It is important to note that, unlike the statistics produced by the Decennial Census, these are all estimates, which means that they have a margin of error—sometimes a fairly large one, especially for small geographic areas. Aggregate ACS data is available through multiple interactive online interfaces, including American FactFinder (http://factfinder2.census.gov, covered in chapter 2) and the Integrated Public Use Microdata System (IPUMS, https://usa.ipums.org/; see appendix B for more information on working with the SDA software used by IPUMS).

Current Population Survey (www.bls.gov/cps/). This survey, conducted by the Census Bureau on behalf of the Bureau of Labor Statistics (BLS), is one of the best sources for socioeconomic data on individuals and households in the United States. It provides the raw data behind many common statistics, most notably the unemployment rate. The core questions on the Current Population Survey—basic demographic, educational, and employment information—are asked every month, and then supplemental sets of questions are asked one month per year. The Annual Social and Economic (ASEC) supplement, sometimes called the "March supplement" since it is administered every March, asks detailed questions about how much education people have completed, what kind of job they have, how many hours they work per week, how much they earn, whether they receive certain government benefits and the value of those benefits, their health insurance status, how much they paid in federal and state taxes, and other questions related to the household's income and expenses. Because of this, it is a favorite source among people with an interest in researching economic inequality, employment discrimination, poverty, and similar topics. Some aggregate data from the Current Population Survey is available on the BLS site (www.bls.gov/cps/). Users who need aggregate data not available from the BLS can use the IPUMS to create tables from CPS data, 1962 to present, in an interactive online interface, after completing a free registration (https://cps.ipums.org/cps/; see appendix B for more information on working with the SDA software used by IPUMS). For the most advanced uses, raw CPS data can be downloaded from the Census Bureau (http://thedataweb.rm.census.gov/ftp/cps_ftp.html), 1994 to present, or from the National Bureau of Economic Research (NBER), 1962 to present (www.nber.org/data/current-population-survey-data.html).

Consumer Expenditure Survey (www.bls.gov/cex/). This survey is also conducted by the Census Bureau on behalf of the BLS. Its focus, as its name suggests, is consumer spending: how much money do Americans spend on food, clothing, shelter, transportation, health care, education, entertainment, and the like? Tables containing this data are available from 1984 to present. Spending data is available broken down by many individual and household variables, including number of people in the household; region in which the household is located; whether the household is in a rural or urban area; income of the household; and age, race, gender, education level, and occupational category of the "reference person" (the person who owns or rents the dwelling for the household). Microdata from the Consumer Expenditure Survey is also freely available online (www.bls.gov/cex/pumdhome.htm), after a 2012 change in procedures. As of the time of this writing, only the 2004–2011 microdata was available online, but eventually the data should be available 1996 to present, with a one-year lag.

American Time Use Survey (ATUS, www.bls.gov/tus). Carried out by the Census Bureau under the sponsorship of the BLS, this survey asks Americans 15 years and older how much time they spent on a single, selected day carrying out activities in dozens of categories, including sleeping, working for pay, volunteering, watching television, exercising, and doing many separate kinds of domestic tasks: caring for children, caring for adults in the household, grocery shopping, preparing food, caring for one's lawn and garden, and exterior maintenance on one's house. Because this data set has such detailed breakdowns of domestic activities, it is a favorite among researchers and pundits interested in gender inequality in the amount of time spent doing this sort of unpaid work. As with the other BLS/Census Bureau surveys, data is available both in tables and charts and as freely available microdata, 2003 to present.

National Center for Health Statistics
(U.S. Centers for Disease Control)

The major official demographic data source for the United States is the National Center for Health Statistics' National Vital Statistics System (www.cdc.gov/nchs/nvss.htm), which collects and disseminates birth and death data from administrative records, namely, birth and death certificates. This data is available in a variety of ways, including published tables and an interactive database called VitalStats. It is a particularly strong source for data on fertility rates and on the deaths of fetuses and infants.

MAJOR SOURCES: WORLD

National and Regional Sites

Many countries conduct household surveys that focus on socioeconomic status (income, expenditure, social inclusion, etc.), but very few of them make the microdata from those surveys freely available as the U.S. Census Bureau does with the Current Population Survey and the Consumer Expenditure Survey. Among the countries and international organizations that make available English-language aggregate data on household incomes and expenditures are the following:

- The European Commission includes detailed aggregate data from its European Union Labour Force Survey and Household Budget Surveys in the Eurostat database (http://ec.europa.eu/eurostat; see chapter 2). Eurostat also contains some data from time-use surveys.
- In the United Kingdom, a great deal of aggregate data from the Expenditure and Food Survey, Family Resources Survey, Labour Force Survey, and other household surveys can be downloaded from the website of the Office for National Statistics (www.ons.gov.uk/ons/datasets-and-tables/index.html).
- For Australia, the aggregate data from the Household Expenditure Survey and the Survey of Income and Housing is available from the Australian Bureau of Statistics (www.abs.gov.au).
- New Zealand allows the interactive creation of tables for data from its Household Economic Survey through the NZ.Stat online tool (www.stats.govt.nz, "Browse for stats" tab).

Census Bureau (U.S. Department of Commerce)

The U.S. Census Bureau's International Programs (www.census.gov/population/international/data/index.html) includes several demographic data resources, most notably the International Data Base (IDB). The IDB provides demographic data for hundreds of countries, territories (e.g., American Samoa, British Virgin Islands), and regions (e.g., Micronesia, Caribbean). Available data sets include population, both total and broken down by age and gender; rate of population growth; data about births, including number, rate per 1,000 population, and births per woman; data about mortality, including life expectancy, infant mortality, and number and rate of deaths; and data about the number of migrants and rate of migration. This database includes both historic data going back to 1950 and projections that currently go out to 2050.

United Nations Statistics Division

The United Nations Statistics Division publishes the annual *Population and Vital Statistics Report* (http://unstats.un.org/unsd/demographic/products/vitstats/), which contains current data on the total, male, and female population of each country, as well as data about the numbers of births, total deaths, and infant deaths. Although the printed and full PDF version is released only once per year, some of the online data tables are updated much more frequently.

MINOR SOURCES

Office of Immigration Statistics
(U.S. Department of Homeland Security)
Migration Policy Institute

Migration data for the United States is available from several sources. Official statistics for documented immigrants to the United States are available via the Department of Homeland Security's Office of Immigration Statistics (www.dhs.gov/data-statistics/). The Migration Policy Institute's Immigration Data Hub (www.migrationinformation.org/data-hub/) is also a good source for basic statistics about immigration both around the world and in the United States.

Office of Population Research (Princeton University)

One of the best sources for microdata about immigration is the Office of Population Research at Princeton University (http://opr.princeton.edu), which disseminates data from several research projects that focus on immigration. These include the following:

Mexican Migration Project (MMP, http://mmp.opr.princeton.edu/home-en.aspx). Since 1982, this project has interviewed people in more than one hundred communities in Mexico about their experiences traveling to the United States or to other parts of Mexico to find work. The survey also gathers detailed demographic information on the households, as well as other general information. Additional interviews have been done with people from those communities who have settled permanently in the United States. Microdata from all of the surveys, now covering more than 20,000 households and nearly 140,000 people, is available.

Latin American Migration Project (LAMP, http://lamp.opr.princeton.edu). This project, which branched off from the MMP in 1998, uses similar methods to examine migration experiences in the rest of Latin America. Currently it has interviewed people from communities in Puerto Rico and ten countries in Central and South America and the Caribbean.

Immigrant Identity Project (IIP, http://opr.princeton.edu/archive/iip/). This data set contains transcribed interviews with 159 first- and second-generation immigrants living in New York City, Philadelphia, and New Jersey.

New Immigrant Survey (NIS, http://nis.princeton.edu). This survey asks legal immigrants to the United States about their experiences with work, education, health, child rearing, and other topics.

Princeton's Office of Population Research also disseminates data from older (generally mid to late twentieth century) surveys and research projects related to fertility, including the World Fertility Survey, the European Fertility Project, and Chinese In-Depth Fertility Surveys. Registration is required to access many of these data sets.

Center for Demography of Health and Aging
(University of Wisconsin–Madison)

The Center for Demography of Health and Aging (www.ssc.wisc.edu/cdha/projects.html), a project of the University of Wisconsin–Madison, makes available both the microdata and reports containing aggregate data from several of its studies. These include the Wisconsin Longitudinal Study, which is following more than 10,000 people from their high school graduation in 1957 until their deaths, and three studies of health and medical care among the elderly in various countries: Health, Wellbeing and Aging in Latin America and the Caribbean, which covers seven Latin American countries; the Mexican Health and Aging Study; and the Puerto Rican Elderly Health Conditions study. Registration is required to access the microdata from many of these surveys.

Bureau of Labor Statistics (U.S. Department of Labor)

The BLS runs longitudinal surveys through its National Longitudinal Surveys program (www.bls.gov/nls/). Over the years four groups, beginning as teenagers or young adults, have been followed: a group of men from 1966 to 1981, a group of women from 1968 to 2003, a mixed-gender group since 1979, and another group since 1997. Additionally, two groups were followed beginning in middle age (a group of men from 1966 to 1990, and a group of women from 1967 to 2003), and in 1988 the study began following the children of the women from the 1979 mixed-gender group. Although the focus is on work experience, consistent with the BLS mission, the surveys also feature questions on education, health status, and personal finances, among other topics.

Panel Study of Income Dynamics (University of Michigan)

The Panel Study of Income Dynamics (PSID, http://psidonline.isr.umich.edu) is another longitudinal study that has followed multiple generations of the same families. The PSID started with five thousand families in 1968 and is still following those families and their descendants today. Additionally, members of families that immigrated to the United States after 1968 were added to the panel in the 1990s. As the name suggests, a major focus of the survey is on family finances, such as employment and expenditures, but there are also questions on health, children, and education. Some of the variables are available only in restricted-use data files, but much of the data is freely available after registration.

Census Bureau (U.S. Department of Commerce)

The Survey of Income and Program Participation (SIPP, www.census.gov/sipp/index.html) is a household-level, longitudinal study managed by the Census Bureau. The focus of this survey is on the economic situation of households, and on how that situation is affected by benefits from various government programs and private not-for-profit organizations, including rent subsidies, free or reduced-price school lunches, and food from charitable organizations. Thus, the survey includes detailed questions about dozens of different potential sources of income, including income from employment, pensions, and child support payments as well as from programs ranging from Social Security to college scholarships. Individuals are also asked questions about their assets and expenditures. SIPP has been ongoing since 1984, but the same people have not been followed for the entire course of the survey; a new panel of households is added, and an old one is dropped, every few years.

Data Sharing for Demographic Research
(Interuniversity Consortium for Political and Social Research)

Data Sharing for Demographic Research (DSDR, www.icpsr.umich.edu/icpsrweb/DSDR/) is a data archive within the Interuniversity Consortium for Political and Social Research (ICPSR). It contains more than five hundred data sets, many of them freely available but some available only to ICPSR subscribers.

AfriPop
AsiaPop

AfriPop (www.clas.ufl.edu/users/atatem/index_files/AfriPop.htm) and AsiaPop (www.asiapop.org) provide fine-grained population density data—people per approximately 100 meters squared—for countries in Africa and Asia, respectively. This data is available as GeoTIFF image files, which can be viewed as is or imported into GIS software for further analysis.

21
Political Science—Elections

IN THIS CHAPTER, THE SOURCES FOR DATA ON ELECTIONS address two phases of the election process: the campaign portion, with data on how money is raised and spent by campaigns, and the voting portion, with data on the number of votes received by each candidate. A third aspect of election-related data, public opinion about candidates and issues, is not covered in this chapter; these sources are reviewed in chapter 24.

MAJOR SOURCES: UNITED STATES

Federal Election Commission

Official campaign finance data for the United States is available from the Federal Election Commission (FEC, www.fec.gov/pindex.shtml). Since the 1970s, candidates and campaign committees have been required to disclose campaign donations from individual donors that exceed a certain threshold (currently $200). The FEC, which oversees this disclosure process, has made available much of the data collected via the candidates' and committees' disclosure filings, which include the donor's name, address, employer, occupation, and date and amount of the donation for each donation to the campaign over the threshold. Microdata about other types of campaign contributions and campaign spending, such as contributions from or independent expenditures by political action committees (PACs), is also included. The FEC has processed data from election cycles since 2008 to make them more user-friendly and easily searchable, with graphical presentations of the data and point-and-click browsing options. Other data goes as far back as the early 1990s. Some of this data is extremely raw, in spreadsheets with cryptic codes rather than human-readable labels, although summary tables and graphical representations are available for some of the older data. This data is extremely rich: it is possible to download a single file with all three-million-plus campaign contributions over $200 that were made during the 2011/12 election cycle, for example.

The FEC also publishes data on election results for federal offices. Official totals for presidential and congressional elections 1982 to present are available on its website (www.fec.gov/pubrec/electionresults.shtml/). These results are not geographically detailed; the presidential results are broken down by state, but the congressional results are not broken down geographically at all.

Center for Responsive Politics

The Center for Responsive Politics, a not-for-profit organization, has set out to create a more user-friendly interface to the FEC campaign finance data, OpenSecrets (www.opensecrets.org). A particular advantage of the OpenSecrets interface is its aggregation of campaign donations by the donors' employers, which allows one to see at a glance that, for example, employees of the University of California collectively donated more than $1 million to Barack Obama's 2012 reelection campaign, beating out the employees of Microsoft Corporation (the second-largest group of donors) by almost $400,000. Although information about donors' employers, and the ability to search by employer, is available through the FEC interface, users would have to calculate the total donated by employees of each business or other institution themselves. OpenSecrets has also cross-referenced campaign contributions and lobbying expenses with earmarks, allowing users to see how much money members of Congress are earmarking for companies whose employees and PACs have donated money to their campaigns. A selection of other information available on the OpenSecrets site includes the net worth of members of Congress and other government officials, information about former politicians who are now working as lobbyists and vice versa, and information about spending by lobbying firms, PACs, and 527 groups.

National Archives and Records Administration

The National Archives and Records Administration (NARA) has state-level election results for U.S. presidential elections from 2000 to the present, and it has national vote totals and electoral vote counts for every U.S. presidential election (www.archives.gov/federal-register/electoral-college/, "Historical Election Results" tab). The Constituency-Level Election Archive, discussed below, has overall results for U.S. congressional elections 1788 to present.

Harvard Election Data Archive
State Secretaries of State

Because of the decentralized nature of American elections, county-level and precinct-level election returns are not available from official federal sources, even for presidential or congressional elections. Precinct-level voting data is available for presidential, congressional, and gubernatorial elections from the 2000s to the present (the exact years vary by state) via the Harvard Election Data Archive (http://projects.iq.harvard.edu/eda/). This data is primarily designed for use in GIS software, although it is also compatible with Excel and some statistical software. Another option for precinct-level or county-level data for federal elections, and often the only option for data for state legislatures and local elected offices, is state secretaries of state. These officials are in charge of overseeing most elections at the state level, and most of them have election data from recent elections available in some format—be it PDFs, spreadsheets, or HTML tables—on their websites. URLs for all of the secretaries of state are available from the National Association of Secretaries of State (www.nass.org/contact/sos-members/), and Wikipedia maintains a list of links to all state's election results pages as well as information about the time periods covered by each state's page (search Wikipedia for "List of United States official election results by state").[1]

MAJOR SOURCES: WORLD

International Institute for Democracy and Electoral Assistance

There are few user-friendly, high-quality, global resources for data on elections. One is the unified database created by the International Institute for Democracy and Electoral Assistance (International IDEA, www.idea.int/uid/). This database is a centralized, easily searchable source of both quantitative and qualitative information about the state of democracy in any given country. More than one hundred indicators measure everything from the fee for filing a complaint about alleged election-related misdeeds to whether the country has compulsory voting. The most extensive data is on campaign finance, with forty-three indicators covering restrictions on campaign donations, public funding of political campaigns, campaign spending limits, campaign finance reporting requirements, and enforcement of campaign finance laws. There is also detailed information on the presence and structure of gender quotas for national and subnational legislatures, as well as information on voter turnout as far back as 1945, legal provisions for referenda, type of electoral system, and rules for challenging election results.

Constituency-Level Elections Archive

Another excellent source for raw data about elections, both U.S. and foreign, is the Constituency-Level Elections Archive (CLEA, www.electiondataarchive .org). It contains data at the level of the electoral district for legislative elections (i.e., congressional or parliamentary elections) in more than eighty countries. More than a thousand elections are included, stretching back to the eighteenth century (for the United States) or the nineteenth century (for Belgium, Canada, Denmark, Iceland, the Netherlands, Norway, Sweden, Switzerland, and the United Kingdom) in some cases. However, elections from the most recent few years are generally not included, and the site is not appropriate for users who are not statistically sophisticated; the only access to the data is through downloaded files in SPSS and Stata formats.

Electoral Institute for Sustainable Democracy in Africa
Political Database of the Americas (Georgetown University)

There are no comprehensive, freely available global sources for data from nonlegislative elections, but there are some regional options. The Electoral Institute for Sustainable Democracy in Africa (EISA, www.eisa.org.za) is a not-for-profit group that promotes good election practices by, among other activities, monitoring elections. It hosts an archive of election results for twenty-two African countries, including both quantitative data (election results) and qualitative data such as reports from its election monitoring teams. Georgetown University's Center for Latin American Studies has created an archive of data about the politics of Latin American countries, the Political Database of the Americas (PDBA Resource, http://pdba.georgetown .edu, "Resources" tab). Among its components are several decades of election results for the countries of Latin America.

MINOR SOURCES

National Electoral Commissions

Campaign finance disclosure laws vary widely across countries, and not all nations have sites equivalent to the FEC in the United States. Sites that do provide detailed campaign finance information at the national level include the Electoral Commission in the United Kingdom (https://pefonline.electoralcommission.org.uk), which has data on donations and campaign expenditures going back to 2001 and data on loans back to 1987, covering political parties, certain elected officials and candidates, and other political groups; the Australian Electoral Commission (www.aec.gov.au), which has financial disclosure reports from political parties back to the 1996 elections and from large donors back to 1998; and Elections Canada, which has data back to 1993 for political parties and to 1997 for candidates (http://elections.ca).

NOTE

1. Comprehensive nationwide election returns at the county or precinct level before 2000 are difficult to come by from free sources. The range of data made available on the state secretaries' of state websites varies widely; data for some states is available all the way back to the nineteenth century, but other states have online data only for the most recent decade or two. Paid resources containing geographically detailed historical election data for the entire United States include the Interuniversity Consortium for Political and Social Research (ICPSR), in the United States Historical Election Returns Series; Dave Leip's Atlas of U.S. Presidential Elections (http://uselectionatlas.org); the CQ Voting and Elections Collection (http://library.cqpress.com/elections/); and the *America Votes* series, which has been published by the Governmental Affairs Institute and Congressional Quarterly since 1956.

22

Political Science—War and Peace

THE STUDY OF WAR, PEACE, AND VIOLENT POLITICAL CONflicts is not an area with considerable quantitative data. No UN office releases any large amount of such data, and although the U.S. Department of Defense publishes a great deal of quantitative information about its own operations, it maintains no central portal that brings all of that information together in one easily searchable place.[1] Nevertheless, a few private organizations and research projects with an interest in war and peace have created some quite useful data sets.

MAJOR SOURCES: WORLD

Stockholm International Peace Research Institute

The Stockholm International Peace Research Institute (SIPRI) produces five databases (www.sipri.org/databases) with both quantitative and qualitative information about war and peacekeeping. The more quantitative of these databases include the Multilateral Peace Operations Database, covering 2000 to present, which contains information such as name and location of the peacekeeping operation, date on which the operation began, names of the countries contributing personnel to the operation, number of various types of personnel (military troops, military observers, civilian police, and other civilian staff) authorized and actually sent, cost of the operation, and number of deaths both annually and overall. Its Military Expenditure Database records the amount of money and percentage of GDP that countries spent on their militaries since 1988, and its Arms Transfers Database contains extensive data on the international sale of weapons going back to 1950. It also hosts a cooperative database, Facts on International Relations and Security Trends (FIRST), which brings together qualitative and quantitative data from more than a dozen organizations with interests in human rights, peace, and democracy. In addition to data from SIPRI's databases, other indicators available in the FIRST database include the Corruption Perception Index (from Transparency International), the Failed States Index (from the Fund for Peace), the Worldwide Press Freedom Index (from Reporters without Borders), and the Global Peace Index (from Vision of Humanity), among others.

Uppsala Conflict Data Program

The Uppsala Conflict Data Program (UCDP, www.pcr.uu.se/research/UCDP/), another participant in the FIRST database, maintains several data sets on armed conflicts. These cover everything from formally declared wars between two governments, to undeclared wars between informal groups of nonstate actors (from ethnic or religious groups to drug cartels), to organized acts of military violence against civilians. In addition to basic information about each conflict—identities of the parties, dates the conflict started and ended—the data sets also contain estimates of the number of people killed in the conflicts. There are also separate data sets on external supporters of combatants in the conflicts. The various data sets cover different time periods, with the oldest going back to 1946.

Correlates of War

One of the best sources for quantitative data about historical conflicts is the Correlates of War project (www.correlatesofwar.org), through which political science faculty and graduate students at several different universities have been collecting standardized data about international conflicts, civil wars, and the factors that may contribute to them since 1963. Most of the data covers the period from 1816 (the end of the Napoleonic Wars) until a few years ago (the ending date varies by data set). Although the data contains many variables that are obviously and directly war related—such as the start and end dates of the conflict, who was fighting, who won and lost, and the number of fatalities—there are also country-level data sets on topics that may influence a country's decision to join or to continue to fight a war. These include the percentage of the country's population belonging to different religions, its membership in intergovernmental organizations, its production of iron and steel, the number of personnel in the armed forces, its military spending, and its military alliances. The data that is not specifically conflict related is reported for countries every year, whether or not they were involved in a war that year. The one drawback to this data is that it is released only as raw data sets, so it is unwieldy for a patron who just wants to know, for example, how much a single country was spending on its military in a given year.

Center for Systemic Peace

The Integrated Network for Societal Conflict Research (INSCR, www.systemicpeace.org/inscr/inscr.htm), a project of the Center for Systemic Peace, distributes data sets about various forms of political violence and about situations that may lead to political violence, such as states that are at risk of failing. Many of the data sets have relatively long time series; the data sets "Major Episodes of Political Violence" and "Coups d'Etat" go back to 1946, and several other data sets, including ones on refugees, genocides, and ethnic war, begin in the 1950s or 1960s. Data from INSCR is available only in Excel and SPSS formats.

Global Terrorism Database (University of Maryland)

The Global Terrorism Database (GTD, www.start.umd.edu/gtd/), hosted by the University of Maryland, contains data about terrorist attacks from 1970 until the present, with a lag of approximately two years. The data includes structured information about various aspects of each attack: group that perpetrated the attack, place of the attack (city, province, country, and region), date of the attack, type of attack (bombing, hijacking, assassination, etc.), target of the attack (private citizens, the military, the government, aviation, etc.), number of people killed and injured, whether hostages were taken, information about property damage from the attack, and more. The data can be accessed in two ways: users can search or browse by specific criteria, or the entire data set can be downloaded for analysis. The results of searching and browsing are presented both in tables and in charts and graphs. Tables with up to one thousand results can be downloaded without restriction, but a free registration is required to download the entire data set or large portions of it.

Empirical Studies of Conflict (Princeton University)

Another university-based project is Empirical Studies of Conflict (http://esoc.princeton.edu), which has detailed conflict-related data for the countries of

Afghanistan, Colombia, Iraq, and Pakistan, and some data for the Philippines and Vietnam. This data includes information about violence of various types (terrorist attacks, military actions, etc.), drug production and anti-drug enforcement, as well as some survey and demographic data; note that not all types of data are available for all countries. Much of the data is georeferenced for use in GIS software, including the information about incidents of terrorism.

Terrorism and Preparedness Data Resource Center

(Interuniversity Consortium for Political and Social Research)

The Interuniversity Consortium for Political and Social Research (ICPSR) at the University of Michigan hosts the Terrorism and Preparedness Data Resource Center (www.icpsr.umich.edu/icpsrweb/TPDRC/), which contains microdata about politically motivated crimes including domestic terrorism, international terrorism, and assassinations. The data sets are rich and varied, including topics such as public opinion about terrorism, steps that various institutions have taken to prepare for terrorist attacks, crime and safety in schools, and collective memories of terrorist attacks. However, a significant number of the data sets are available only to ICPSR subscribers, which can make the database frustrating to search for people not affiliated with ICPSR member institutions. Still, some potentially useful data sets are freely available.

NOTE

1. There are a nontrivial number of data sets from the Department of Defense in Data.gov (covered in chapter 2).

23
Political Science—Other

IN ADDITION TO THE PROJECTS MENTIONED IN CHAPTER 22, SEVeral others in other areas of political science have worked to code nonnumeric data about politics to facilitate quantitative analyses of such information. This coding process results in spreadsheets and other datasets that record information about political activities, from State of the Union addresses to political rallies, in a structured, machine-readable format.

MAJOR SOURCES: UNITED STATES

Policy Agendas Project

The Policy Agendas Project (www.policyagendas.org) creates data sets that allow for rigorous analyses of changes in the U.S. federal government's priorities, as well as certain nongovernmental factors, such as public opinion and media coverage, that help to drive those changes. The project has released several separate data sets for different types of political activities, such as congressional hearings, bills introduced in Congress, congressional roll call votes, State of the Union addresses, and executive orders. Each action is coded as related to one of the hundred-plus areas in which the federal government makes policy, from unemployment to federal holidays. Thus, users of these data sets can analyze when and why a given issue is discussed or acted upon more or less frequently by various branches of government. An online graphing tool allows less statistically inclined users to simply visualize the changes over time.

Supreme Court Database

The Supreme Court Database (http://scdb.wustl.edu) has coded all cases heard before the Supreme Court from 1946 until the most recent completed Court term on 247 different variables, covering everything from the chronology of the case to the legal issues it raised. The data can be downloaded in many different formats, and it can be analyzed and visualized online in a user-friendly interface. Want to see a chart showing the number of Supreme Court cases involving civil rights by year? From the "Analysis" page, two clicks gets you there.

Fraser Institute
Mercatus Center
(George Mason University)

Two libertarian-leaning organizations, the independent Fraser Institute in Canada and the Mercatus Center at George Mason University in Virginia, rate all fifty U.S. states on their policies in a variety of areas. The Fraser Institute's Free the World.com site (www.freetheworld.com/index.php), which is primarily focused on economic freedom, also rates the provinces of Canada and provides national and subnational rankings for many other countries. The Mercatus Center's Freedom in the 50 States site (http://freedominthe50states.org) provides ratings in a variety of areas, including fiscal policies such as taxes and government spending; regulatory policies that impact economic freedom, such as restrictions in the markets for health insurance and cable television; and policies that impact personal freedom, such as restrictions on alcohol, marriage, and campaign finance. The Mercatus Center also publishes the raw data it uses to create its rankings (www.statepolicyindex.com/the-research/).

MAJOR SOURCES: WORLD

DataGov (Inter-American Development Bank)

DataGov (www.iadb.org/datagob/) is an extraordinarily comprehensive database of "governance indicators"—that is, variables that provide evidence of how democratically a country is governed and how well civil society and the rule of law function in that country. DataGov includes a few hundred such indicators, ranging from the extent of bribery in the country's educational system to the freedom of the country's press. The data is gathered from a wide range of sources, including Freedom House's (www.freedomhouse.org) *Freedom in the World: The Annual Survey of Political Rights and Civil Liberties*, Transparency International's (www.transparency.org) *Global Corruption Barometer*, the Heritage Foundation/*Wall Street Journal* Index of Economic Freedom (www.heritage.org/index/), and several other similar publications and databases. Although DataGov is produced by the Inter-American Development Bank, which primarily focuses on Latin America, it includes data for all countries of the world for many variables.

Polity Project

The Polity Project (www.systemicpeace.org/polity/polity4.htm) is a long-running effort; it has been publishing data sets since the 1970s. Although the Polity data is distributed by the Integrated Network for Societal Conflict Research (INSCR, see chapter 22), it deserves separate mention here because of its focus on internal governance. For every country with a population over 500,000 and for every year since 1800, the data set contains a small set of indicators of the democratic and authoritarian status and the political stability of the country. These indicators include the presence/absence of an orderly, institutionalized process for choosing the chief executive; the extent of legal restrictions on the country's chief executive; and ratings of the competitiveness and openness of the political process.

Global Database of Events, Language, and Tone Computational Event Data System

Several projects that code information about international conflict and violent terrorist attacks are mentioned in chapter 22. In addition to those projects, there have also been several similar efforts to code information about less violent or purely domestic events, such as strikes, protest marches, and domestic assassinations. The data sets created by these projects typically include structured information about such topics as the parties involved in the event, type of event (e.g., rally, bombing, government crackdown), and date and place of the event.

The most notable example may be the Global Database of Events, Language, and Tone (GDELT, http://gdeltproject.org). GDELT has assembled a large data set, covering nearly all countries of the world from 1979 to yesterday and containing hundreds of millions of events. New events are added every day.

This feat is accomplished by using software to code news stories automatically rather than have human coders read and code the stories.

Another automated-coding project for this type of data is the Computational Event Data System (http://eventdata.parusanalytics.com), a descendent of an even older automated coding project, the Kansas Event Data System (KEDS). As KEDS and then as the Penn State Event Data Project, these data sets have been under construction since the early 1990s. Data sets covering specific areas—such as the Balkans, the Persian Gulf region, West Africa—and specific time periods are available.

24
Public Opinion Surveys

STATISTICS RESULTING FROM PUBLIC OPINION SURVEYS AND political polls are available seemingly everywhere: in journal articles, in the popular press, and even on the Web. There are, however, far fewer free sources for public opinion or polling *data*. This chapter reviews the notable exceptions.

MAJOR SOURCES: UNITED STATES

American National Election Studies
(Stanford University and the University of Michigan)
General Social Survey
(National Opinion Research Center at the University of Chicago)

Both the American National Election Studies (ANES, www.electionstudies .org) and the General Social Survey (GSS, www3.norc.org/gss+website/) are venerable surveys: ANES surveys have been conducted every two years since 1948 (with additional pilot studies in some odd years), and the GSS has been run either annually or biennially since 1972. The questions on ANES cover a wide range of topics, both directly and indirectly related to American politics and elections. For example, questions include feelings toward various political, religious, and socioeconomic groups (e.g., unions, the military, Catholics, conservatives), appraisals of the presidential candidates in presidential election years, and opinions about the socioeconomic situation of African Americans, to name just a few of the broad topics covered. In general the GSS covers people's opinions on social issues ranging from family relationships to socioeconomic inequality, although some of the topic areas and questions change every year. Both surveys can be analyzed online through the SDA Archive at the University of California–Berkeley (http://sda.berkeley.edu/archive.htm; see appendix B for instructions for using the SDA software).

Odum Institute for Research in Social Science

(University of North Carolina at Chapel Hill)

The Odum Institute for Research in Social Science maintains an extensive catalog of public opinion data sets (http://dvn.iq.harvard.edu/dvn/dv/odum/). Many, but not all, of these data sets are freely available to the public. One valuable collection consists of data from more than one thousand surveys from Harris Interactive and its predecessor Louis Harris and Associates, dating back to 1958. This polling organization conducted surveys on a wide range of topics, primarily political opinion polls but also surveys about health and nutrition, public education, and more. Other notable data sets include data from *USA Today* and *Atlanta Journal-Constitution* polls from the 1980s and early 1990s and the National Network of State Polls, which contains several hundred polls that were conducted in a single U.S. state.

MAJOR SOURCES: WORLD

Consortium of European Social Science Data Archives

The Consortium of European Social Science Data Archives (CESSDA) maintains the CESSDA Catalogue (www.cessda.net/catalogue/), which allows users to search for survey data from the national social science data archives of many European countries. A wide range of social and economic topics, from politics and social policy to sports, nature, and the media, are covered in the various surveys. Most of the data is from the 1980s to present, but some older surveys are available. Although the catalog itself is centralized, access to the data is via the websites of each of the national data archives. This leads to differences in accessibility between different data sets; for example, some data and interfaces are available in English, others only in the official language of the country or the original language of the survey. Access to some of these data archives requires registration. Many of the individual archives allow their data to be analyzed online using the NESSTAR software (www.nesstar.com), which provides similar functions to the SDA software commonly used for online analysis by American data archives but has a very different interface.

Globalbarometer Surveys

The Globalbarometer Surveys encompass four different ongoing survey projects: the Afrobarometer (www.afrobarometer.org; conducted since 1999), Arabbarometer (www.arabbarometer.org; conducted since 2006), Asian Barometer (www.asianbarometer.org; conducted since 2001; data available by application only), and Latinobarómetro (www.latinobarometro.org; conducted since 1995; there is a charge for the most recent year's data, but older years are free).[1] These surveys are a rich source of data on people's opinions about politics and public life in participating countries, with special emphasis on opinions about democracy, trust in various institutions, and participation in civic life. The Arabbarometer can be downloaded only in SPSS format; the Afrobarometer can be downloaded in SPSS format or analyzed online; and the Latinobarómetro can be downloaded in SPSS, SAS, or Stata format or analyzed online. All four projects, including the Asian Barometer, also publish freely available reports containing statistics generated from the data.

World Values Survey

The World Values Survey (www.wvsevsdb.com) is a lengthy public opinion survey that has been conducted in more than fifty countries, many of which have been surveyed multiple times since the project was launched in 1981. Many of the questions are similar to those on the Globalbarometer Surveys, covering people's opinions on politics and democracy (e.g., "How important is it for you to live in a country that is governed democratically?") and their trust in various groups and institutions, but there are also sections with more personal questions about people's religious beliefs and opinions about family life (e.g., "How important is God in your life?"). Data from the World Values Survey has been merged with data from the European Values Survey (www.europeanvaluesstudy.eu), a separate project whose maintainers cooperated with the maintainers of the World Values Survey to generate harmonized data sets, to create an even larger sample. This integrated data set is available on the World Values Survey website.

MINOR SOURCES

Pew Research Center

The Pew Research Center is an umbrella organization encompassing seven different ongoing research projects. Data sets are available from many of the Pew Research Center's subdivisions (http://pewresearch.org/databank/

datasets/), including the weekly surveys conducted by the Pew Research Center for the People and the Press, the National Survey of Latinos by the Pew Research Hispanic Center, international surveys from the Pew Research Global Attitudes Project, and assorted surveys on other topics, including those performed by the Pew Research Internet and American Life Project and the Pew Research Forum on Religion and Public Life. Most of the available data is from the 2000s, with only the Pew Research Center for the People and the Press data going as far back as 1997. Registration is required for access to some of the data.

Latin American Public Opinion Project

The Latin American Public Opinion Project (LAPOP) at Vanderbilt University (www.vanderbilt.edu/lapop/) has performed the AmericasBarometer survey every two years since 2004. The survey has been administered at least once in every Central and South American country as well as in some Caribbean nations. Despite its name, it is not part of the Globalbarometer Surveys project, but it asks similar questions, focusing on people's opinions about democracy, their involvement in politics and civic life, and their trust in various people and institutions, from the president of their country to the Catholic Church. Data can be analyzed online or downloaded in Stata or SPSS formats.

CBS News Polls

One source for polling statistics (not raw data sets) that is worth mentioning is the online archive of CBS News polls (www.cbsnews.com/news/cbs-news-poll-database/). This freely available database contains thousands of questions that have been asked on public opinion surveys sponsored by CBS News since 1976. Questions can be browsed by topic or searched by keyword, and the responses are presented graphically as well as in tables.

NOTE

1. Although the Eurobarometer survey, which is available through the CESSDA Catalogue, is similar to the other Barometer surveys, it is not part of the Globalbarometer project.

25
Transportation

THIS CHAPTER CONTAINS SOURCES FOR DATA ON ALL MODES OF transportation—public transportation, private motor vehicles, trains, airplanes, ships, and even pipelines—moving both people and cargo. Some data about automobile production and sales is included in this chapter, but additional data about the automotive industry can be found in the sources in chapter 10. Data about transportation fatalities are included in this chapter. For data on fuels used for transportation, see chapter 18.

MAJOR SOURCES: UNITED STATES

Bureau of Transportation Statistics
(U.S. Department of Transportation)

The Bureau of Transportation Statistics (BTS, www.rita.dot.gov/bts/), part of the U.S. Department of Transportation, publishes detailed statistics on the movement of both people and cargo, both within the United States and across its borders. The BTS site can be used to access not just BTS data but also data reported by other units of the federal government, such as highway statistics from the Federal Highway Administration, air travel data from the Federal Aviation Administration, and statistics on maritime transportation from the Maritime Administration. Because the BTS does not host the data reported by other agencies, only links to it, the site can be confusing for novice users; each agency presents its own data in a different interface and format. The total amount of aggregate data and statistics available is, however, vast. It includes information about such subjects as the number of miles of roads in the United States and the number of passengers flying annually along with detailed data about delayed and canceled flights, the funding of public transit systems, and the busiest days for ferry trips, to name just a few. Historical data is available; some of the highway statistics are available back to the 1940s, and data about aircraft accidents is available back to 1962, for example.

MAJOR SOURCES: WORLD

United Nations Economic Commission for Latin America and the Caribbean
United Nations Economic Commission for Asia and the Pacific
United Nations Economic Commission for Europe

The United Nations does not have an agency equivalent to the U.S. Department of Transportation and does not report statistics on most transportation-related topics in UNdata or other centralized sites, but three of the regional United Nations Economic Commissions do gather and disseminate transportation statistics.

The Economic Commission for Latin America and the Caribbean (ECLAC), through its CEPALSTAT database (http://estadisticas.cepal.org), reports total number of motor vehicles, number of motor vehicles per 100 residents, total length of roads in the country, total length of railways in the country, and three indicators of the volume of air traffic: total number of kilometers flown, number of passenger-kilometers flown, and ton-kilometers of freight flown.

Similarly, the Economic Commission for Asia and the Pacific (ESCAP) has a Data Centre (www.unescap.org/stat/data/) with indicators such as density of roads and railroads, percentage of roads that are paved, number of cars per 1,000 residents, raw number of highway deaths and number per 100,000 residents, kilometers of road in the country that are part of the Asian Highway network, volume of cargo and passenger traffic on railroads, and volume of shipping containers being loaded and unloaded at ports in the country.

The Economic Commission for Europe (UNECE) Statistical Database (http://w3.unece.org/pxweb/Dialog/) includes detailed country-level statistics on the movement of people and goods by motorcycles, passenger cars, buses, trains, and boats; number, age, engine size, load capacity, and fuel (diesel, gasoline, electricity, natural gas, liquefied petroleum gas, or other) of various types of vehicles (cars, buses, trucks, motorcycles); length of various types of roads and the length and density of various types of railways; traffic accidents, broken down by the conditions, type of accident, and more, as well as statistics on number of deaths and injuries per 100,000 automobiles; number and power of electric, diesel, and steam locomotives; number, age, and carrying capacity of boats and ships; and number and gender of people employed by railroads, either in administration or operations. Most data goes back to the early 1990s.

MINOR SOURCES

Organisation for Economic Co-operation and Development

For developed countries, the Organisation for Economic Co-operation and Development's OECD.StatExtracts (http://stats.oecd.org) contains national-level data similar to that found in the United Nations Economic Commission databases, including annual passenger-kilometers by various types of transportation (train, car, and bus); annual freight ton-kilometers by rail, roads, inland waterways (rivers, lakes, canals, etc.), seas, and oil pipelines; number and tonnage of containers transported by sea and by rail; and number of road accidents causing injuries, number of people injured, and number of people killed. One advantage of OECD.StatExtracts is that most of this data is available back to 1970.

Census Bureau (U.S. Department of Commerce)

Over the years the Census Bureau has asked several questions, first on the Decennial Census long form and now on the American Community Survey, about people's commuting patterns. These questions include what type of transportation people use to get to work, how long their commute takes, what time they leave for work at the beginning of their day, and where their job is located.[1] Because of the geographic detail of this type of data, it can be useful for people interested in studying local rush-hour traffic patterns. See chapter 2 for more information about accessing data from the Census Bureau.

A discontinued data series from the Census Bureau, the Vehicle Inventory and Use Survey (www.census.gov/svsd/www/vius/products.html; formerly known as the Truck Inventory and Use Survey), is still a valuable source for those interested in historic data about transportation in the United States. This survey asked the owners of trucks—a category that includes pickup trucks, minivans, and sport utility vehicles as well as commercial vehicles such as tractor-trailers, dump trucks, and cargo vans—questions about the vehicle's physical characteristics and about how it was acquired, used, and maintained. Microdata—individual users' responses to the survey questions—is available every five years from 1977 to 2002, and aggregate data is also available for 1963 and 1967.

Public Transportation Data

Several cities, both in the United States and abroad, have made their own public transit data publicly available. Two kinds of transit data are commonly shared: data on stops, routes, and schedules; and ridership statistics. The data on stops, routes, and schedules is typically disseminated in General Transit Feed Specification (GTFS) format, which was developed to make it easy for apps and websites to make use of this data to help people plan their trips. The inclusion of latitudes and longitudes for stations and bus stops allows this data to be used in GIS software. Extensive lists of transit data available in GTFS format are available on the GTFS Data Exchange site (www.gtfs-data-exchange.com) and on the GoogleTransitDataFeed project (http://code.google.com/p/googletransitdatafeed/). Some cities, such as San Francisco (https://data.sfgov.org), also make available other geographically coded transportation information, such as the locations of parking meters and speed limits for streets. Chicago is a good example of a city that makes ridership statistics available; in the City of Chicago Data Portal (https://data.cityofchicago.org) one can find the exact number of people who rode a bus on any given bus route for any given day since January 1, 2001. That's over half a million lines of data!

National Automobile Dealers Association

The automotive industry is a major part of the American economy with numerous associated industry groups, some of which publish statistics on their particular corner of the industry. These include the National Automobile Dealers Association (NADA), which publishes annual NADA DATA reports (www.nada.org) covering such topics as sales of new cars, used cars, and parts and service; dealerships' gross sales and net profits; vehicle inventories; numbers, types, and earnings of employees at dealerships; and dealership advertising methods and expenses. Much of this data is available at the state level, and new vehicle sales are available broken down by manufacturer. The reports from 2002 to present have been published online.

Organisation Internationale des Constructeurs d'Automobiles

Internationally, the Organisation Internationale des Constructeurs d'Automobiles (OICA, also known in English as the International Organization of Motor Vehicle Manufacturers, http://oica.net), a trade association for automotive companies, collects statistics on the production of four classes of motor vehicles (passenger cars, light commercial vehicles, heavy commercial vehicles, and buses), broken down by country and by manufacturer, 1997 to present. OICA also publishes sales data, broken down by country and by cars versus all commercial vehicles, 2005 to present.

WardsAuto

WardsAuto (http://wardsauto.com) is one of the best private sources for data on the automotive industry, both in the United States and internationally. The vast majority of its data is available by subscription only, but a few useful historical data sets are available publicly: number of cars and trucks sold in the United States, 1931 to present (although data is missing for 1942–1950); number of cars and trucks produced in North America, 1951 to present; and the market share for thirty-seven different automotive companies, 1961 to present.

NOTE

1. The responses to the final question are typically recoded before they are released, usually into a variable such as whether they work in the same county or the same "place" (Census jargon for city, town, village, etc.) that they live.

26
Spatial Data

MANY OF THE DATA SOURCES COVERED IN PREVIOUS CHAPters contain data with a geographic component—data that is available by country, by province, by U.S. Census tract, or data that consists of observations at a single point, such as a weather station. As users of GIS know, this data can easily be displayed and analyzed in a GIS framework. The sources in this chapter specifically provide data that is useful only in the context of GIS, such as georeferenced satellite images of the earth or shapefiles of points and polygons that can be interpreted only by GIS software. Thus, if you are helping patrons who wish to do spatial analyses, it is often necessary to consult both this chapter for GIS-specific data and the relevant subject chapter for more widely usable social, economic, environmental, or other data that is available by geography.

MAJOR SOURCES: UNITED STATES

Data.gov (U.S. General Services Administration)

This federal data catalog (www.data.gov), which is covered more fully in chapter 2, allows users to search an impressive amount of geographic data. As of the time of this writing, the National Oceanic and Atmospheric Administration (NOAA) was the largest contributor, with more than 32,000 of its spatial data sets included in the Data.gov catalog. The next largest contributor is the National States Geographic Information Council (NSGIC), a private organization whose members include staff from state, local, and federal agencies that deal with GIS data. Prior to the launch of Data.gov, NSGIC created a "GIS Inventory" site (http://gisinventory.net) that collected metadata about geographic data sets from these state and local agencies, allowing users to cross-search the data made available by all of the contributing agencies. The inclusion of the contents of this GIS Inventory in the Data.gov catalog allows users to search not just federally created geographic data but state and local geographic data as well. In addition, several states and state agencies are contributing metadata for geospatial data sets directly to Data .gov without going through the NSGIC GIS Inventory.

U.S. Geological Survey (U.S. Department of the Interior)

Although the Geological Survey (USGS) has contributed thousands of geographic data sets to Data.gov, it also hosts two of its own geospatial data portals, one with geographic data only for the United States and one that covers the world. The U.S.-only portal, The National Map (http://nationalmap .gov), primarily provides access to basic geographic data such as elevation; land cover; roads; cities and counties; locations of airports, hospitals, schools, and other types of structures; and boundaries of watersheds. Some additional data about land cover, natural hazards such as floods and wildfires, and conservation status is also available. Some data is available both as shapefiles and as geodatabases; other data can be downloaded as GeoTIFFs. To access data, users draw a bounding box on a map and then select from a list of data available for their selected area. Access is not instantaneous; users must provide an e-mail address and wait anywhere from a few seconds up to two days to receive an e-mail with a link to download their selected data.

The other portal, EarthExplorer (http://earthexplorer.usgs.gov; free registration required to download data), covers the entire globe. It provides more advanced users access to many types of data, particularly a great deal of aerial photography and satellite imagery. Much of the latter was collected by satellites launched by the National Aeronautics and Space Administration (NASA), such as the Landsat satellites, and some of this data can also be accessed via NASA websites (see chapter 5).

MAJOR SOURCES: WORLD

INSPIRE Geoportal (European Union)

The INSPIRE Geoportal (http://inspire-geoportal.ec.europa.eu) provides access to hundreds of thousands of geographic data files produced by various public and private organizations in Europe. Although the sponsors of the data are European, some of the available data covers geographic areas beyond the European continent. A majority of the data sets include purely geographic or cartographic information—place names, political boundaries, elevation, base layers—but there are also hundreds of data sets on social, economic, and environmental issues. A great deal of care has been given to make the site function well in a multilingual environment. Keyword searches are automatically expanded to include synonyms in multiple languages; a multinational thesaurus, the General Multilingual Environmental Thesaurus (GEMET), is used to translate certain keywords into multiple languages, and all of the translated keywords are automatically included in the search. Once a language has been selected, a translation widget provides a machine translation of the metadata into the user's chosen language.

MINOR SOURCES

Center for International Earth Science Information Network (Columbia University)

The Center for International Earth Science Information Network (CEISEN) is different from most of the other sources in this chapter; it does not primarily provide base layers and other purely geographic data. Instead, it hosts programs and projects that provide GIS data in a variety of subject areas. One of these projects, the NASA Socioeconomic Data and Applications Center (SEDAC), is notable for providing GIS-formatted, gridded data sets based on various data sets collected by other organizations. Many of these are based on environmental data, including data sets on greenhouse gas emissions drawn from data from the Intergovernmental Panel on Climate Change. Other environmental data sets provide species distribution information for birds and mammals in the Americas, and amphibians globally, based on data from NatureServe. Another group of data sets, "Last of the Wild," has gridded data about geographic areas with the most and the least amount of human impact, as measured by the Human Footprint Index and the Human Influence Index. There is also gridded data about the population of the United States based on demographic information from the U.S. Census, and about the population of the world based on data from the United Nations and country-level censuses.

National Historical Geographic Information System
(Minnesota Population Center)

The National Historical Geographic Information System (NHGIS, www.nhgis .org; free registration required) is one of several excellent sources for historical demographic information for the United States run by the Minnesota Population Center. (Another, the Integrated Public Use Microdata Series, is mentioned in chapter 20.) This site allows users to download demographic, agricultural, and other data from the Decennial Census and other surveys run by the U.S. Census Bureau from 1790 to present. Crucially, the site also provides users shapefiles indicating the boundaries of states, counties, cities, ZIP codes, Census tracts, and so on as they existed at the time the data was collected, which makes it possible to use the historical data easily and accurately with GIS software.

U.S. Department of Agriculture

The U.S. Department of Agriculture (USDA) operates the Geospatial Data Gateway (http://datagateway.nrcs.usda.gov), which allows users to download spatial data for counties, states, and other regions of the United States. Although the data is distributed by the USDA, only some of the data—such as information about soils, orthophotographs that are part of the National Agricultural Imagery Program, and raster data about crops grown—is directly about agriculture. Other available data covers such topics as demographic and housing information, average precipitation and temperatures, land cover, conservation easements, and hydrography.

27

When All Else Fails

Using Article Databases, WorldCat, and Real Live People to Find Data

MAYBE YOU HAVE FLIPPED THROUGH THIS BOOK, LOOKING FOR a likely source to find an obscure data set, and none of the listed sources seems quite right. Or maybe it seems obvious that a particular agency ought to report the data your patron needs, but you cannot find it anywhere on the agency's website. What now?

ARTICLE DATABASES

Although listed here under "When All Else Fails," articles are often a good place to *start* looking for statistics, and they can also provide useful pointers to data sets. Some scholars calculate new statistics in their research and report them in academic journals. A good example of this is health research, which generates all manner of statistics that seek to quantify how various actions—taking a particular drug, eating particular foods, or performing certain types of exercise, for example—affect a person's risk for various conditions. Statistics such as these generally do not appear in the databases listed in the previous chapters in this book; often, finding the articles in which these statistics were originally reported is the only way to access them.

Scholarly and popular articles can also be useful as pointers toward both statistics and data sets. Often scholars cite statistics calculated by others, or perform analyses on data sets constructed by others, in the course of making their arguments. In the popular press, journalists report on newly released statistics, and op-ed columnists refer to the same statistics to support their opinions. Depending on the patron, their purposes, and the type of article in which the statistics were found, the article itself may be enough to answer the question. If not, the citation to the statistics or the data set used to create them can provide useful clues about which government agency or private research group collects the necessary data.[1]

Articles can also be useful in confirming that certain data does not exist. Finding several recent articles by reputable scholars lamenting that they cannot do a particular analysis because the necessary data has not been collected or has been lost is powerful evidence that the data, in fact, is not available. For example, the U.S. Census Bureau does not ask questions about people's religious affiliation. This omission makes it difficult to arrive at accurate estimates for the population of adherents of smaller religions in the United States, a fact that is frequently noted by scholars who would like demographic information about American Muslims.

WORLDCAT

WorldCat is a terrible place to look for specific data points, but for certain types of historical data that have not been digitized it can be the best—and, sometimes, only—clue that the data you need might be available in print. The free-floating Library of Congress Subject Headings subdivision "statistics" can be used to identify statistical publications (e.g., *International Financial Statistics Yearbook*, published by the International Monetary Fund, or *Vital Statistics of the United States*, published by the National Center for Health Statistics), and combining the free-floating subdivisions "statistics" and "periodicals" can help to identify the holy grail for those in search of historical time-series data—an annual publication that used a consistent methodology to publish annual data for an extended period of time. For example, the scholar interested in changes in causes of death in various regions of Sri Lanka over the past thirty years will likely be frustrated by the lack of data available on the Web but heartened to see that several American institutions hold copies of the series *Annual Health Bulletin, Sri Lanka*—which can be found with a subject search for "Public health—Sri Lanka—Statistics—Periodicals."

REAL LIVE PEOPLE

If you know which agency ought to be responsible for collecting a specific type of data, that information can help you find a real, live person to consult if you cannot find the necessary data online. Most U.S. federal agencies that disseminate data have clear instructions on their websites for contacting them for further information about that data, and the federal site USA.gov also maintains a directory with contact information for federal agencies (www.usa.gov/directory/federal/index.shtml). Don't be shy about contacting these agencies with questions. Several agencies have librarians or other staff assigned specifically to help the public use their data. One example is the Census Bureau, which maintains networks of state data centers (www.census.gov/sdc/network.html) and regional offices (www.census.gov/regions/) that assist with data dissemination and use. These state and regional offices can be a valuable resource for finding specific Census data about your local area. Similarly, the Bureau of Labor Statistics has regional information offices (http://bls.gov/bls/regncon.htm). But even agencies without such dedicated information offices are still generally happy to answer questions about their data. After all, the scores of statisticians, scientists, economists, and other experts who spent years working within these agencies to develop this data want the data to be used.

Another excellent resource is your colleagues in the library profession. There are several open library-related electronic discussion lists where data reference questions are frequently asked. These include GOVDOC-L (http://govdoc-l.org), a list for librarians working with government information, and LPSS-L, the electronic discussion list of the Law and Political Science Section of ACRL. Librarians who wish to become more involved in data reference might even consider joining LPSS or one of the other organizations devoted to data services librarianship, such as the International Association for Social Science Information Services and Technology (IASSIST, www.iassistdata.org) or the ACRL Numeric and Geospatial Data Services in Academic Libraries Interest Group. As data reference continues to become a more important part of the services offered by many libraries, participating in organizations such as these will allow you to help shape the future of this area of librarianship.

NOTE

1. This assumes that there is an actual citation. Articles in the popular press typically provide only imprecise references to the source of the data (e.g., "New unemployment figures released today by the Bureau of Labor Statistics"), and, unfortunately, the references in scholarly articles are often not much clearer; see appendix A for more information about current and proposed standards for citing data in scholarly publications. But even knowing the name of the agency that produced the data can often be enough of a pointer to launch a successful data search.

APPENDIX A

Citing Data

NONE OF THE MAJOR CITATION STYLES—CHICAGO, APA, AND MLA—in their current editions provide explicit guidelines for citing data sets. For the one area in which they do provide explicit guidance—citing tables of data from an external source—they provide guidance that is far from ideal, many data librarians believe. These style guides recommend citing the source of the data only in a note on the table. A better way of citing data, some librarians have argued, would be to cite it along with textual sources in footnotes or bibliographies, where the data citations can easily be indexed and used by resources that take citations into account, such as Web of Science and Google Scholar. Citing the data only in a note on the table effectively hides the data citations from research tools that are limited to citations in the footnotes or bibliographies.[1]

Several organizations of data librarians and data users have been working to promote better standards for data citation. These include the Special Interest Group on Data Citation (SIGDC) of the International Association for Social Science Information Services and Technology (IASSIST, www.iassistdata

.org) and DataCite (www.datacite.org), an international effort with members including the Digital Curation Center in the United Kingdom (www.dcc.ac.uk) and the Australian National Data Service (www.ands.org.au).

IASSIST has produced "Quick Guide to Data Citation," a freely reproducible, Creative Commons–licensed handout that provides clear and useful advice to students who would like to cite their data effectively and responsibly while still generally conforming to a recognized citation style such as MLA or APA. The following advice is copied directly from that handout.

EXCERPT FROM "QUICK GUIDE TO DATA CITATION"

Elements of Data Citation

Author: Name(s) of each individual or organizational entity responsible for the creation of the dataset.

Date of publication: Year the dataset was published or disseminated.

Title: Complete title of the dataset, including the edition or version number, if applicable.

Publisher and/or distributor: Organizational entity that makes the dataset available by archiving, producing, publishing, and/or distributing the dataset.

Electronic Location or Identifier: Web address or unique, persistent, global identifier used to locate the dataset (such as a DOI). Append the date retrieved if the title and locator are not specific to the exact instance of the data you used.

These are the minimum elements required for dataset identification and retrieval. Fewer or additional elements may be requested by author guidelines or style manuals. Be sure to include as many elements as needed to precisely identify the dataset you have used.

For Example

Arrange these elements following the order and punctuation specified by your style guide. If examples for datasets are not provided, the format for books is generally considered a generic format that can be modified for other source types.

APA (6th edition)

Smith, T.W., Marsden, P.V., & Hout, M. (2011). *General social survey, 1972-2010 cumulative file* (ICPSR31521-v1) [data file and codebook].

Chicago, IL: National Opinion Research Center [producer]. Ann Arbor, MI: Interuniversity Consortium for Political and Social Research [distributor]. doi: 10.3886/ICPSR31521.v1

MLA (7th edition)

Smith, Tom W., Peter V. Marsden, and Michael Hout. *General Social Survey, 1972-2010 Cumulative File.* ICPSR31521-v1. Chicago, IL: National Opinion Research Center [producer]. Ann Arbor, MI: Inter-university Consortium for Political and Social Research [distributor], 2011. Web. 23 Jan 2012. doi:10.3886/ICPSR31521.v1

Chicago (16th edition) (author-date)

Smith, Tom W., Peter V. Marsden, and Michael Hout. 2011. *General Social Survey, 1972-2010 Cumulative File.* ICPSR31521-v1. Chicago, IL: National Opinion Research Center. Distributed by Ann Arbor, MI: Inter-university Consortium for Political and Social Research. doi:10.3886/ICPSR31521.v1

"Quick Guide to Data Citation." International Association for Social Science Information Services & Technology (IASSIST), 2012. Retrieved May 16, 2014, from www.iassistdata.org/sites/default/files/quick_guide_to_data_citation_high-res_printer-ready.pdf. Used under a Creative Commons Attribution 3.0 license: http:// creative commons.org/licenses by/3.0/.

NOTE

1. Heather Piwowar, who tweets at @researchremix, is a good source to follow for updates on the issues mentioned in this paragraph.

APPENDIX B

Getting Started with the Survey Documentation and Analysis Software

SURVEY DOCUMENTATION AND ANALYSIS (SDA) IS OPEN-source software that is used for online dissemination of data from many surveys and censuses, including the U.S. Decennial Census, the American Community Survey, and the Current Population Survey, all of which are collected by the U.S. Census Bureau and distributed through the Integrated Public Use Microdata Series (IPUMS). SDA is also used to disseminate data from large ongoing research projects such as the General Social Survey and the American National Election Study (see chapter 23). SDA allows users to do many types of statistical analyses (regressions, correlations, etc.) on data sets without downloading the data or using a desktop statistical program such as SPSS or Stata. For reference librarians, its most useful feature is its ability to make custom tables, called "crosstabulations" in statistics jargon.

Only website administrators can load data sets into SDA, so you can analyze a data set with SDA only if an organization such as IPUMS or the Interuniversity Consortium for Political and Social Research (ICPSR) has that data set up for SDA access. Look on these organizations' websites for links that say something such as "Analyze data online" or "Analyze data using SDA."

On many of these sites, you are asked to create a free account, log in, and agree to certain terms of use before accessing the data via SDA.

By default, SDA should open in the "Frequencies/Crosstabulations Program," which allows you to create tables. If you are an advanced user and want to do other types of analyses, such as correlations or regressions, you can access those options under the "Analysis" menu in the upper left. This guide does not cover those analyses.

In SDA, the variables are listed in the left column, and the table-building options are in the right column (see figure 1). The first step is to find the variables you need in the left column. If you want more information about any given variable, click on it; this copies the variable name into the "Selected" box at the top of the left column. Then click the "View" button next to the "Selected" box to see details about the variable. These details may include the full text of the question asked and always include the possible responses and the numeric codes used for each response (see figure 2).

To use a particular variable in constructing your table, close the "View" window and click one of the "Copy to" buttons underneath the "Selected" box. There are four "Copy to" buttons, one for each of the options for using a variable in constructing a table. "Row" and "Column" simply place that variable in either the rows or the columns of the table. "Control" creates separate tables for each of the possible values for that variable. For example, using "sex" as the control variable creates separate tables with the responses for men and women (assuming that the survey had a variable named "sex" with that information). "Filter" allows you to limit which groups are included

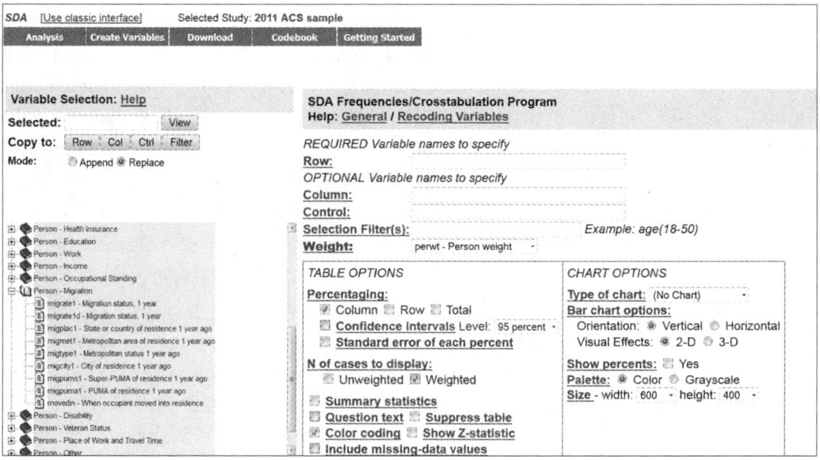

FIGURE 1

in the table. For example, instead of using "sex" as a control variable, you could use it as a filter variable and view only the responses of women.

The final variable-related option in SDA is "Weight." Many surveys use weight variables to compensate for the fact that their surveys are not simple random samples. If you have ever taken an introductory statistics course, you probably remember your professor emphasizing that the tests you learned were appropriate only for samples randomly chosen from the population, where every person in the population had an equal chance of being selected to be in the study. Few large data sets in the social sciences satisfy this requirement. Thus, since some people have a higher or lower likelihood of participating in the survey, it is appropriate to give their answers more or less weight when calculating statistics that are intended to represent the entire population. Weight variables are used to accomplish this. Often, the survey is set up in SDA to use a weight variable already, in which case you do not need to change anything. Nevertheless, it is always a good idea to look at the weight variable options and make sure that the selected one makes sense. This is especially important when working with multilevel data such as the U.S. Census data, which uses different weight variables for individual-level data (e.g., age, educational attainment) and household-level data (e.g., household income).

There are several "Table Options" and "Chart Options" for changing the format of and adding additional information to the output from SDA. Much of this additional information is intended for more statistically sophisticated users and can safely be ignored when answering the typical "Can you help me

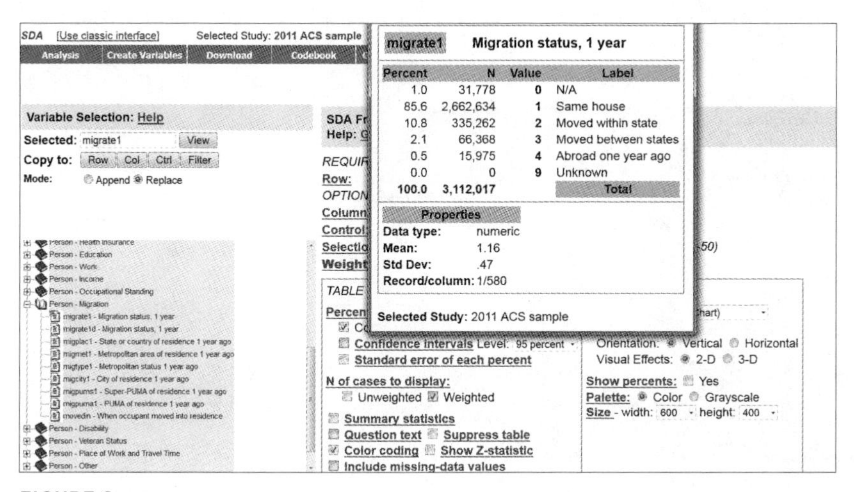

FIGURE 2

find a table with this information?" type of data reference question. Many of the other options are self-explanatory, such as including the question text or changing the type of chart created. If you are curious about any of these options, just click on its name to get more information.

The exception is "Confidence interval." In my opinion, it is always a good idea to add the confidence interval to your table. The statistics calculated by SDA are estimates, and they come with a margin of error. If you are working with a small sample (which can easily happen if you use the "filter" option to examine a small subset of the population—say, only people living in Delaware, or only people over age 50 with advanced degrees), the margin of error can be quite large. Selecting "confidence interval" as an option adds (depending on your selection) the 90%, 95%, or 99% confidence interval to each cell in the table. This confidence interval, which is presented as a range, gives you information about the precision of each estimate.

For example, I used data from the 2011 American Community Survey, as disseminated through IPUMS, to examine the phenomenon of retirees moving to Florida's gulf coast. When I looked only at people age 65–70 who lived in the city of Cape Coral (which has a city code of "1000" in this data set), SDA produced an estimate that 91.4 percent of those senior citizens are living in the same house they lived in one year ago; 5.0 percent had moved from another house in Florida in the past year; 2.8 percent had moved from a house in a different state in the United States, and 0.7 percent had moved from a foreign country (see figures 3 and 4). However, the 95% confidence intervals for those estimates are wide. For example, although the estimate is that 2.8 percent of the 65–70-year-olds living in Cape Coral had moved there from another state in the previous year, the 95% confidence interval is 1.0–8.1 percent. That means that there is a 95 percent chance that the true

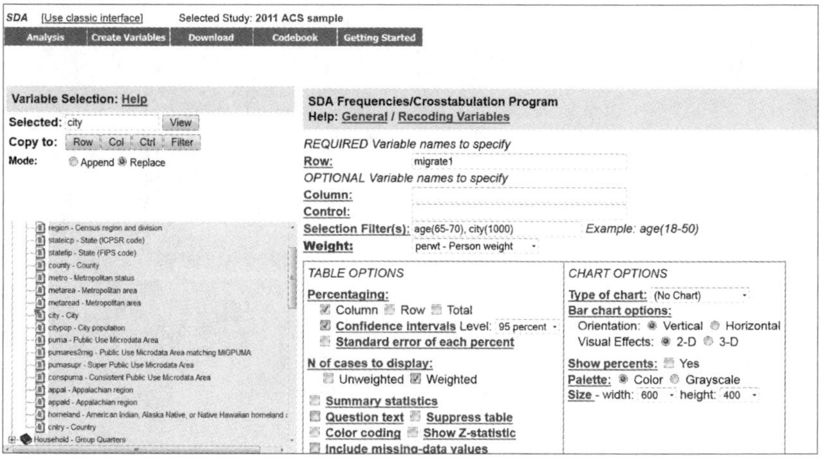

FIGURE 3

figure—the percentage you would find if you asked this question of every single 65–70-year-old living in Cape Coral—is somewhere between 1.0 and 8.1 percent, and a 5 percent chance that the true figure is less than 1.0 percent or greater than 8.1 percent.

Compare this to the 95% confidence interval if one generates the same table for people age 65–70 living in the entire state of Florida. In this case, the estimate is 2.6 percent, but the 95% confidence interval is 2.4–2.9 percent

2011 ACS sample

Jan 14, 2013 (Mon 09:30 AM CST)

Variables					
Role	**Name**	**Label**	**Range**	**MD**	**Dataset**
Row	**migrate1**	Migration status, 1 year	0-4		1
Weight	**perwt**	Person weight	1.00-2,471.00		1
Filter	**age(65-70)**	Age	0-95		1
Filter	**city(1000)**	City(=Cape Coral, FL)	0-7590		1

Frequency Distribution		
Cells contain: -**Column percent** -Confidence intervals (95 percent) -Weighted N		**Distribution**
migrate1	1: Same house	**91.4** *(84.7-95.4)* 11,684.0
	2: Moved within state	**5.0** *(2.2-10.9)* 643.0
	3: Moved between states	**2.8** *(1.0-8.1)* 364.0
	4: Abroad one year ago	**.7** *(0.1-6.0)* 90.0
	COL TOTAL	***100.0*** --- *12,781.0*

FIGURE 4

(see figure 5). Even the 99% confidence interval is only 2.3–3.0 percent. For the entire state of Florida, we can say with near-complete confidence that the percentage of the population age 65–70 who moved from another U.S. state to Florida last year is between 2.3 and 3.0 percent. For the city of Cape Coral, we can be much less confident about the true percentage.

When you have selected all the options you want, click the "Run the Table" button to create your data table.

2011 ACS sample

Jan 14, 2013 (Mon 09:33 AM CST)

Variables					
Role	**Name**	**Label**	**Range**	**MD**	**Dataset**
Row	**migrate1**	Migration status, 1 year	0-4		1
Weight	**perwt**	Person weight	1.00-2,471.00		1
Filter	**age(65-70)**	Age	0-95		1
Filter	**statefip(12)**	State (FIPS code)(=Florida)	1-56		1

Frequency Distribution		
Cells contain: -**Column percent** -Confidence intervals (95 percent) -Weighted N		**Distribution**
migrate1	1: Same house	**91.8** *(91.3-92.2)* 1,079,072.0
	2: Moved within state	**4.7** *(4.4-5.1)* 55,508.0
	3: Moved between states	**2.6** *(2.4-2.9)* 30,824.0
	4: Abroad one year ago	**.9** *(0.7-1.0)* 10,142.0
	COL TOTAL	***100.0*** --- *1,175,546.0*

FIGURE 5

Index

A

ACRL Numeric and Geospatial Data Services in Academic Libraries Interest Group, 149
administrative data, 5, 11
African Development Bank Group (AFDB), 18
AfriPop, 118
Afrobarometer, 135
Agency for Healthcare Research and Quality (AHRQ), 106
aggregate data, 4
Air Facility System Search, 39
Air Quality System (AWS), 39
AirBase, 42
AirCompare, 39
AirData, 39
ALA Guide to Economics and Business Reference, 58
ALFRED (Archival Federal Reserve Economic Data), 49
Altinok, Nadir, 97
America Votes, 123n1
American Community Survey (ACS), 16, 93, 111–112, 139, 155, 158
American FactFinder, 14, 57, 82
American Housing Survey, 81–82
American National Election Studies (ANES), 133–134, 155
American Time Use Survey (ATUS), 113
AmericasBarometer, 136
Annual Retail Trade Report, 56
Annual Services Report, 56, 60
Annual Social and Economic (ASEC) supplement, 112
Annual Survey of Manufactures, 14, 56–57, 62

Annual Survey of Public Employment and Payroll, 52
Annual Survey of Public Pensions, 52
Annual Survey of State and Local Government Finances, 14, 52
Annual Wholesale Trade Report, 56
ANSS Comprehensive Earthquake Catalog, 32
APA guidelines, 152–153
AQS Data Mart, 39
Arabbarometer, 135
Arms Transfers Database, 126
article databases, 147–148
Aruoba-Diebold-Scotti Business Conditions Index, 49
Asian Barometer, 135
Asian Development Bank, 18, 48–49
AsiaPop, 118
Association of Southeast Asian Nations (ASEAN), 87
ASTER, 35
Atlanta Journal-Constitution, 134
Atlas of U.S. Presidential Elections, 123n1
ATSR World Fire Atlas, 35
Australian Bureau of Statistics, 59, 114
Australian Electoral Commission, 123
Australian Institute of Health and Welfare (AIHW), 109
Australian National Data Service, 152
Australian Prudential Regulation Authority (APRA), 78–79

B

Bank for International Settlements (BIS), 78, 82
Beginning Teacher Longitudinal Study, 95
Behavioral Risk Factor Surveillance System (BRFSS), 106
Boston College, 95–96
Broad Economic Categories (BEC), 89
Budget of the United States Government, 53
Bureau of Economic Analysis (BEA), 7, 71–72, 85, 87
Bureau of Justice Statistics (BJS), 7, 28, 30
Bureau of Labor Statistics (BLS), 7, 14, 65–68, 111–113, 116–117, 149
Bureau of Transportation Statistics (BTS), 7, 137–138

C

Carbon Dioxide Information Analysis Center (CDIAC), 40–41
Case, Karl, 83
CBS News Polls, 136
Census Bureau. *See* U.S. Census Bureau
Census of Agriculture, 22
censuses, 5
Center for Demography of Health and Aging, 116
Center for International Earth Science Information Network (CEISEN), 145
Center for Latin American Studies, Georgetown University, 122
Center for Responsive Politics, 120
Center for Systemic Peace, 127
Centers for Disease Control (CDC), 103, 106, 113–114
CEPALSTAT/Databases and Statistical Publications, 18–19, 138
CESSDA Catalogue, 134–135, 136n1
Charity Navigator, 60
Chicago Manual of Style, 153
Chinese In-Depth Fertility Surveys, 116
City of Chicago Data Portal, 140
classification codes, 6–7
Climate Change Convention, 41
Climate.gov, 38, 40
Columbia University, 145
ComCat, 32
Comext, 91
Committee on Payment and Settlement Systems (CPSS), 78
Commodity Trade Statistics Database (UNSD), 48
Computational Event Data System, 131–132
Comtrade (Commodity Trade Statistics Database), 88, 89
confidence interval, 158

Consolidated Federal Funds Report (CFFR), 54n1
Consortium of European Social Science Data Archives (CESSDA), 134–135
Constituency-Level Election Archive (CLEA), 121, 122
Consumer Expenditure Survey, 113, 114
Consumer Financial Protection Bureau (CFPB), 76
Consumer Price Index, 48
Consumer Product Safety Commission, 7
Correlates of War project, 126–127
Corruption Perception Index, 126
County Business Patterns, 10–11, 14, 16, 57
CQ Voting and Elections Collection, 123n1
Crime in the United States, 28
CrimeMapping.com, 30
cross-sectional data, 5
Culture-MERIS, 35
Current Employment Statistics (CES), 66
Current Industrial Reports, 62
Current Population Survey, 10, 14, 68, 93, 112, 114, 155

D

Dartmouth Atlas of Health Care, 108
data
    citing, 151–153
    collection of, 7
    dissemination of, 7–10
    lacuna in, 148
    private collection of, 9–10
    restrictions on collecting, 9
    subtypes of, 4–5
    suppression of, 10–11
    as term, 3–4
Data Archiving and Networked Services (DANS), 29
Data Centre (UNESCAP), 138
Data Finder (EPA), 33–34
data jargon, 3–7
data reference, 1–2
Data Sharing for Demographic Research (DSDR), 117
datacatalogues.org, 19
DataCite, 152
Data.gov, 14–15, 32, 45, 128n1, 143–144
DataGov, 130–131
DataIntal, 91
Decennial Census, 16, 93, 112, 139, 146, 155. *See also* U.S. Census Bureau
Demographic and Health Surveys (DHS), 105
Department of Education (U.K.), 97–98
development banks, regional, 17–19
Digital Curation Center, 152
Drug Abuse Warning Network (DAWN), 107

E

Early Childhood Longitudinal Study, 94–95
Earth Observing System Data and Information System (EOSDIS), 33
EarthExplorer, 32–33, 144
Earthquake Hazards Program, 32
ECA Databank, 18
Economic Census, 14, 56, 57
Economic Commission for Europe (UNECE) Statistical Database, 138–139
Economic Research Service (ERS), 7, 21–22
EDGAR (Electronic Data Gathering, Analysis, and Retrieval), 55–56
EDGAR (Emissions Database for Global Atmospheric Research), 41
EDGAR Online, 58
Elections Canada, 123
Electoral Commission (U.K.), 123
Electoral Institute for Sustainable Democracy in Africa (EISA), 122
Electronic Data Gathering, Analysis, and Retrieval (EDGAR), 55–56
Emissions and Generation Resource Integrated Database (eGRID), 101
Emissions Database for Global Atmospheric Research (EDGAR), 41
Empirical Studies of Conflict, 127–128
Employee Benefits Survey, 67

Employer Cost for Employee Compensation, 67
Employment Cost Index, 67
Employment Projections, 67
Energy Information Administration (EIA), 7, 99–100
Envirofacts, 34
Environmental Marine Information System (EMIS), 45–46
Environmental Protection Agency (EPA), 33–34, 44
Environmental Protection Agency (EPA) Data Finder, 38–39
Eurobarometer, 136n1
European Alien Species Information Network (EASIN), 34
European Commission, 34, 45–46, 53, 114
European Crime and Safety Survey (EU ICS), 29
European Drought Observatory, 34
European Environment Agency, 34–35, 41–42, 45
European Fertility Project, 116
European Forest Data Centre (EFDAC), 34
European Forest Fire Information System (EFFIS), 34
European Labour Force Survey and Household Budget Surveys, 114
European Soil Portal, 34
European Space Agency (ESA), 35
European Union, 17, 145
European Union Open Data Portal, 17
European Values Survey, 135
Eurostat database, 17, 24, 45, 49, 53, 82–83, 114
Expenditure and Food Survey, 114
Exporter Dynamics Database, 90

F

Facility Level Information on Greenhouse Gases Tool (FLIGHT), 39
Facility Registry System, 34
Facts on International Relations and Security Trends (FIRST), 126
Failed States Index, 126
Family Resources Survey, 114
FAOSTAT, 23
FastStats, 104
Federal Aviation Administration, 138
Federal Bureau of Investigation (FBI), 28
Federal Committee on Statistical Methodology, 7
Federal Deposit Insurance Corporation (FDIC), 76
Federal Election Commission (FEC), 119–120
Federal Financial Institutions Examination Council (FFIEC), 76, 77
Federal Highway Administration, 138
Federal Home Loan Mortgage Corporation (Freddie Mac), 83
Federal Housing Finance Agency (FHFA), 83
Federal Reserve Bank of Philadelphia, 49–50
Federal Reserve Bank of St. Louis, 47–48
Federal Reserve Banks, 50
Federal Reserve Economic Data (FRED), 47–48, 66, 75, 83
FedStats, 9
FFIEC Central Data Repository's Public Data Distribution site, 76, 77
Financial Access Survey, 77–78
Financial Times, 58, 63
Fish and Wildlife Service, 7
Floods Portal, 34
Food Aid Information System, 23–24
Food and Agriculture Organization (FAO), 9, 15, 23
Food Availability Data System, 22
Foreign Trade website, U.S. Census Bureau, 86
Foundation Center, 60
FRASER (Federal Reserve Archival System for Economic Research), 49
Fraser Institute, 130
FRED (Federal Reserve Economic Data), 47–48, 66, 75, 83

Freddie Mac (Federal Home Loan Mortgage Corporation), 83
Free the World.com, 130
Freedom House, 131
Freedom in the 50 States, 130
Freedom in the World (Freedom House), 131
Fund for Peace, 126

G

Gapminder, 20
General Certificate of Secondary Education (GCSE), 98
General Multilingual Environmental Thesaurus (GEMET), 145
General Social Survey (GSS), 10, 133–134, 155
General Transit Feed Specifications (GTFS) format, 140
George Mason University, 130
Georgetown University, 122
Geospatial Data Gateway, 146
GIEWS Food Price Data and Analysis Tool, 23
GIS, 141
GIS Inventory site, 144
Global Change Master Directory, 33, 35, 39–40
Global Corruption Barometer (Transparency International), 131
Global Database of Events, Language and Tone (GDELT), 131–132
Global Health Observatory Data Repository, 105
Global Land Cover Facility, 35
Global Marine Information System (GMIS), 46
Global Peace Index, 126
Global Terrorism Database (GTD), 127
Globalbarometer Surveys, 135, 136
GlobCover, 35
Google Earth, 38
Google Public Data Explorer, 20
GoogleTransitDataFeed project, 140
GOVDOC-L, 149
Governmental Affairs Institute and Congressional Quarterly, 123n1
Groningen University, 72
GTFS Data Exchange site, 140

H

Halifax House Price Index, 84
Harmonized System (HS), 7, 89
Harmonized Tariff Schedule (HTS), 88
Harris Interactive, 134
Harvard Election Data Archive, 121
Health, Wellbeing and Aging in Latin America and the Caribbean, 116
Health and Social Care Information Centre, 108–109
Healthcare Cost and Utilization Project (HCUP), 106
Heritage Foundation/*Wall Street Journal* Index of Economic Freedom, 131
Home Mortgage Disclosure Act, 76
House Price Index, 84
House Price Indices, 83
Household Economic Survey, 114
Household Expenditure Survey, 114
Human Footprint Index, 145
Human Influence Index, 145

I

ILOSTAT, 68–69
IMF's Government Finance Statistics (GFS), 53
Immigrant Identity Project (IIP), 116
Immigration Data Hub, Migration Policy Institute, 115
INDSTAT, 48
Industrial Commodity Statistics Database, 62
INSPIRE Geoportal, 145
Institute for Environment and Sustainability (IES), 34, 45–46
Institute for Statistics (UNESCO), 95
Integrated Network for Societal Conflict Research (INSCR), 127, 131
Integrated Postsecondary Education Data System (IPEDS), 94

Integrated Public Use Microdata Series (IPUMS), 146, 155, 158
Integrated Public Use Microdata System (IPUMS), 112–113
Inter-American Development Bank (IDB), 18, 48, 91, 130–131
Intergovernmental Panel on Climate Change, 145
Internal Revenue Service, 7, 59–60
International Association for Social Science Information Services and Technology (IASSIST), 149, 151–152
International Crime Victimization Survey (ICVS), 29
International Data Base (IDB), 114–115
International Energy Agency (IEA), 100–101
International Financial Statistics database (IMF), 48
International Financial Statistics Yearbook (IMF), 148
International Food Policy Research Institute (IFPRI), 24
International Institute for Democracy and Electoral Assistance (International IDEA), 121–122
International Labour Organization (ILO), 9, 15, 68–69
International Monetary Fund, 15, 48, 53, 77–78, 148
International Organization of Motor Vehicle Manufacturers, 141
International Programs, U.S. Census Bureau, 114–115
International Soil Reference and Information Centre, 35
International Standard Industrial Classification (ISIC), 7, 59
International Tariff and Trade Data Web, 88
International Telecommunications Union, 9, 15
International Trade Administration (ITA), 85, 87
Interuniversity Consortium for Political and Social Research (ICPSR), 30, 54n2, 107–108, 117, 123n1, 128, 155
ISRIC—World Soil Information, 35

J

Jean and Alexander Heard Library, Vanderbilt University, 19
Job Openings and Labor Turnover Survey, 67–68
Joint Research Centre (European Commission), 34
Joint United Nations Programme on HIV/AIDS, 9, 15

K

Kansas Event Data System (KEDS), 132
Kellam, Lynda M., 2
Key Indicators of the Labour Market (KILM), 68–69

L

LABORSTA, 68
Labour Force Survey, 114
Land Registry, 84
Landsat, 35, 144
Latin American and Caribbean Macro Watch Data Tool, 48
Latin American Migration Project (LAMP), 116
Latin American Public Opinion Project (LAPOP), 136
Latinobarómetro, 135
Law and Political Science Section of ACRL, 149
Leip, Dave, 123n1
Library of Congress Subject Headings, 148
Livingston Survey, 49
Lloyd's Banking Group, 84
Local Area Unemployment Statistics, 67
local jurisdictions, 29–30
Locality Pay Survey, 70n2
longitudinal data, 5

Longitudinal Employer-Household Dynamics program, 69
Louis Harris and Associates, 134
LPSS-L, 149

M

Maddison, Angus, 73
Maddison Project, 73
Manufacturers' Shipments, Inventories, and Orders, 61–62
Maritime Administration, 138
Medical Expenditure Panel Survey (MEPS), 106
Mercatus Center, 130
Metropolitan Police website, 30
Mexican Health and Aging Study, 116
Mexican Migration Project (MMP), 115–116
microdata, 4, 10
Migration Policy Institute, 115
Military Expenditure Database, 126
Millennium Development Goals, 40, 95
Mineral Resources On-Line Spatial Data, 32
Ministry of Economy, Trade and Industry (Japan), 59
Minnesota Population Center, 16–17, 146
MLA guidelines, 153
MODIS, 35
Monitoring and Future Surveys, 108
Multilateral Peace Operations Database, 125–126
MyWATERS Mapper, 44

N

NADA DATA reports, 140
NAICS codes, 56, 59, 88
NAICS Related-Party database, 86
NASA Socioeconomic Data and Application Center (SEDAC), 145
National Accounts Main Aggregates, 72
National Accounts Official Country Data, 48
National Addiction and HIV Data Archive Program (NAHDAP), 107–108
National Aeronautics and Space Administration (NASA), 33, 35, 39–40, 144, 145
National Agricultural Imagery Program, 146
National Agricultural Statistics Service (NASS), 7, 21–22
National Ambulatory Medical Care Survey (NAMCS), 104
National Archive of Computerized Data on Aging (NACDA), 107, 108
National Archive of Criminal Justice Data, 30
National Archives and Records Administration (NARA), 121
National Assessment of Educational Progress (NAEP), 94
National Association of Realtors (NAR), 83–84
National Association of Secretaries of State, 121
National Automobile Dealers Association (NADA), 140
National Bureau of Economic Research (NBER), 113
National Cancer Institute, 106
National Center for Education Statistics (NCES), 7, 93–95
National Center for Health Statistics (NCHS), 7, 103–105, 107, 113–114
National Center for HIV/AIDS, Viral Hepatitis, STD, and TB Prevention, 106
National Center for Science and Engineering Statistics, 7
National Compensation Survey (NCS), 67, 70n2
National Compensation Survey—Benefits, 67
National Credit Union Administration (NCUA), 76–77
National Crime Victimization Survey, 28
National Emissions Inventory (NEI), 39
National Gap Analysis Program, 32

National Health and Nutrition Examination Survey (NHANES), 25n1, 104, 107
National Health Care Surveys (NHCS), 104–105
National Health Interview Survey (NHIX), 104
National Health Service (NHS; England), 108–109
National Historical Geographic Information System (NHGIS), 14, 16–17, 146
National Home and Hospice Care Survey, 104
National Home Health Aide Survey, 104
National Hospital Ambulatory Medical Care Survey (NHAMCS), 104
National Hospital Care Survey (NHCS), 104
National Hospital Discharge Survey, 104
National Immunization Survey, 105
National Institute of Justice, 30
National Institute on Aging, 108
National Institute on Drug Abuse, 27, 107–108
National Longitudinal Surveys program, 116–117
National Map, The, 33, 144
National Network of State Polls, 134
National Nursing Assistant Survey, 104
National Nursing Home Survey, 104
National Oceanic and Atmospheric Administration (NOAA), 37–38, 45, 144
National Oceanographic Data Center, NOAA, 45
National Opinion Research Center, 133–134
National States Geographic Information Council (NSGIC), 144
national statistical agencies, 19, 59
National Survey of Children with Special Health Care Needs, 105
National Survey of Children's Health, 104–105
National Survey of Family Growth, 104, 107
National Survey of Latinos, 136
National Survey of Residential Care Facilities, 104
National Survey of Substance Abuse Treatment Services (N-SSATS), 107
National Survey on Drug Use and Health (NSDUH), 107
National Vital Statistics System, 104, 113–114
National Water Information System, 43–44
NatureServe, 145
NCES Common Core of Data (CCD), 94, 98
NCHHSTP Atlas, 106
NESSTAR software, 134–135
New Immigrant Survey (NIS), 116
New Zealand Health Survey, 109
New Zealand's Ministry of Health, 109
Nonemployer Statistics, 60n1, 69
Normalized Difference Vegetation Index (NDVI), 35
North American Industry Classification System Codes (NAICS), 6–7
not-for-profit sector, 60
Numeric Data Services and Sources for the General Reference Librarian (Kellam), 2
Nutrition Survey (New Zealand), 109

O

Occupational Employment Statistics (OES), 66–67
Odum Institute for Research in Social Science, 134
OECD.StatExtracts, 17, 24, 139
Office for National Statistics (U.K.), 114
Office of Immigration Statistics, 115
Office of Juvenile Justice and Delinquency Prevention, 30
Office of Population Research, 115–116
Office of Research, Evaluation and Statistics of the Social Security Administration, 7

Office of the Comptroller of the Currency (OCC), 76, 77
Omega Group, 30
Open Knowledge Foundation, 19, 54
OpenSecrets, 120
OpenSpending, 54
Oral Health Survey (New Zealand), 109
Organisation for Economic Co-operation and Development (OECD), 17, 24, 58–59, 78, 91, 95–97, 139
Organisation Internationale des Constructeurs d'Automobiles (OICA), 141
Organization of Petroleum Exporting Countries (OPEC), 87, 100

P

panel data, 5
Panel Study of Income Dynamics (PSID), 117
Penn State Event Data Project, 132
Penn World Table, 72
personal contacts, 148–149
Pew Research Center, 135–136
Pew Research Center for the People and the Press, 136
Pew Research Forum on Religion and Public Life, 136
Pew Research Global Attitudes Project, 136
Pew Research Hispanic Center, 136
Pew Research Internet and American Life Project, 136
Piwowar, Heather, 153n1
Police.uk, 30
Policy Agendas Project, 129–130
Political Database of the Americas (PDBA), 122
Polity Project, 131
population, 5
Population and Vital Statistics Report, 115
preferential trade agreement (PTA) database, 90
Primary Mortgage Market Survey, 83
Princeton University, 115–116, 127–128
privacy, 10–11
Programme for International Student Assessment (PISA), 95–97
Progress in International Reading Literacy Study (PIRLS), 95–96
Projections Central, 70n3
Public Transportation Data, 140
PublicData.eu, 19
public-use data, 4
Puerto Rican Elderly Health Conditions study, 116

Q

Quarterly Census of Employment and Wages (CEW), 66, 67
Quarterly House Price Index, 84
Quarterly Survey of Pubic Pensions, 52
Quarterly Workforce Indicators (QWI), 69
Quotable Value Ltd., 84

R

Real-Time Data Research Center, 49–50
regional development banks, 17–19
regional trade agreement (RTA) database, 90
Reporters without Borders, 126
Reserve Bank of New Zealand, 78–79
Residential Price Index, 84
restricted data, 4
Reverb tool, 33
Roper Center for Public Opinion Research, 136n1
Rosling, Hans, 20

S

S&P/Case-Shiller Home Price Indices, 83
sample, definition of, 5
Schedule B, 7
SDA Archive, 134
SDA software. *See* Survey Description and Analysis (SDA) software
Semiannual Monetary Policy Report, 50
Shiller, Robert, 83
Southern and Eastern Africa Consortium for Monitoring Educational Quality (SACMEQ), 97

Special Interest Group on Data Citation (SIGDC), 151–152
Standard & Poors, 83
Standard Industrial Classification (SIC) code, 56, 88
Standard International Trade Classification (SITC), 7, 88, 89
Stanford University, 133–134
StatBase, 18
state departments of education, 97
state secretaries of state, 121
StatExtracts system, 59
Statistical Abstract of the United States, 14
statistical analysis, 3
Statistical Database System (Asian Development Bank), 49
statistics, description of, 3–4
Statistics New Zealand, 59
Statistics of Income Division of the Internal Revenue Service, 7
Statistics of Income program, 60
statistics reference, 1
Stockholm International Peace Research Institute (SIPRI), 125–126
STORET, 44
Structural Analysis Database (STAN), 58–59
Substance Abuse and Mental Health Data Archive (SAMHDA), 107
Substance Abuse and Mental Health Services Administration (SAMHSA), 27, 107
Supplemental Nutrition Assistance Program (SNAP), 22
Supreme Court Database, 130
Surf Your Watershed tool, 44
Surveillance Epidemiology and End Results Program database (SEER), 106
Survey Description and Analysis (SDA) software, 107, 135, 155–160
Survey of Business Owners (SBO), 57, 60n1, 69
Survey of Credit Underwriting Practices, 77
Survey of Income and Housing, 114
Survey of Income and Program Participation (SIPP), 117
Survey of Professional Forecasters, 49
surveys, 5

T

Tariff Analysis Online (TAO) site, 90
Terrorism and Preparedness Data Resource Center, 128
time-series data, 5
Toxics Release Inventory, 34
Trade in Value Added (TiVA) data set, 91
TradeStats Express (TSE), 87
TRAINS. *See* UNCTAD TRAINS (Trade Analysis and Information System)
Transparency International, 126, 131
Treatment Episode Data Set (TEDS), 107
Trends in International Mathematics and Science Study (TIMSS), 95–96
Truck Inventory and Use Survey, 139

U

UK National Statistics Publication Hub, 59
UNCTAD TRAINS (Trade Analysis and Information System), 88, 89–90
UnctadStat, 25, 63, 88–89
UNdata, 15–16, 40, 48, 62
UNESCAP Data Centre, 138
UNESCO Institute for Statistics, 95
Uniform Crime Reports, 28
unit of analysis, 6
unit of observation, 6
United Nations, 7, 9, 15–16, 44–45
United Nations Children's Fund, 9, 15
United Nations Conference on Trade and Development (UNCTAD), 25, 63, 88–89
United Nations Development Programme (UNDP), 9, 15, 20
United Nations Economic and Social Commission for Asia and the Pacific (UN ESCAP), 19
United Nations Economic and Social Commission for Western Asia, 19

United Nations Economic Commission for Africa (UNECA), 18
United Nations Economic Commission for Asia and the Pacific (ESCAP), 138
United Nations Economic Commission for Europe (UNECE), 18, 138–139
United Nations Economic Commission for Europe (UNECE) Statistical Database, 24–25
United Nations Economic Commission for Latin America and the Caribbean (ECLAC), 18–19, 138
United Nations Educational, Social, and Cultural Organization (UNESCO), 9, 15, 95
United Nations Food and Agriculture Organization (FAO), 23
United Nations Framework Convention on Climate Change (UNFCCC), 9, 15, 41
United Nations High Commissioner for Refugees, 9, 15
United Nations Industrial Development Organization, 9, 16, 48
United Nations Office on Drugs and Crime (UNODC), 9, 16, 28–29
United Nations Population Division, 9, 16
United Nations Regional Economic and Social Commissions, 17–19
United Nations Statistics Division (UNSD), 9, 16, 48, 62, 72, 100, 115
United States Agency for International Development (USAID), 105
United States Historical Election Returns Series, 123n1
universe (population), 5
University of California, 120
University of California–Berkeley, 134
University of California–Davis, 72
University of Chicago, 133–134
University of Maryland, 35, 127
University of Michigan, 30, 117, 128, 133–134
University of Minnesota, 16–17
University of North Carolina at Chapel Hill, 134
University of Pennsylvania, 72
University of Wisconsin-Madison, 116
UN-Water, 44–45
Uppsala Conflict Data Program (UCDP), 126
U.S. Border Control, 29
U.S. Census Bureau, 7, 10–11, 13–14, 16, 51–52, 56–57, 61–62, 68, 69, 81–82, 85, 86, 88, 111, 114–115, 117, 139–140, 145, 146, 148, 149, 155
U.S. Centers for Disease Control. *See* Centers for Disease Control (CDC)
U.S. Customs and Border Protection, 87
U.S. Department of Agriculture (USDA), 21, 146
U.S. Department of Commerce, 13–14, 21, 45, 51–52, 56–57, 69, 71–72, 81–82, 85–87, 111, 114–115, 117
U.S. Department of Defense, 125, 128n1
U.S. Department of Education, 93–95, 97
U.S. Department of Energy, 40–41, 99–100
U.S. Department of Health and Human Services, 106–107
U.S. Department of Homeland Security, 29, 115
U.S. Department of Housing and Urban Development (HUD), 82
U.S. Department of Justice, 28
U.S. Department of Labor, 65–68, 111–113, 116–117
U.S. Department of the Interior, 31–33, 43–44, 144
U.S. Department of the Treasury, 77
U.S. Department of Transportation, 137–138
U.S. Environmental Protection Agency (EPA), 101
U.S. General Services Administration, 14–15, 143–144
U.S. Geological Survey (USGS), 31–33, 43–44, 144

U.S. International Trade Commission, 88
U.S. International Trade Statistics, 86
U.S. National Institutes of Health, 106, 107
U.S. Office of Management and Budget, 52–53
U.S. Securities and Exchange Commission, 55–56, 58
USA Today, 134
USA Trade Online, 88
USA.gov, 149
USAspending, 52–53

V

Vanderbilt University, 19, 136
variables, use of, 156–157
Vehicle Inventory and Use Survey, 139–140
Vision of Humanity, 126
Vital Statistics of the United States, 148
VitalStats, 114
Volcano Hazards Program, 32

W

Wall Street Journal, 131
WardsAuto, 141
Water Information System for Europe (WISE), 45
Watershed Assessment, Tracking and Environmental Results (WATERS), 44
Web-based Injury Statistics Query and Reporting System (WISQARS), 106
weight variables, 157
Wikipedia, 121
Wisconsin Longitudinal Study, 116
World Bank, 16, 48, 73, 90
World Bank Data, 48, 90, 101
World Customs Organization, 7
World Data Center for Atmospheric Trace Gases, 40
World Fertility Survey, 116
World Food Programme, 23–24
World Health Organization, 9, 16, 105
World Integrated Trade Solution (WITS), 89–90
World Meteorological Organization (WMO), 9, 16, 40
World Soil Profiles, 35
World Tourism Organization (WTO), 9, 16
World Trade Organization (WTO), 90, 91
World Values Survey, 135
WorldCat, 148
Worldwide Press Freedom Index, 126

Y

Yahoo! Finance, 58

Z

ZIP Code Business Patterns, 57